What people are saying about …

STAND

"What an amazing message! Marian Jordan Ellis mines the Scriptures to show us why and how we can stand, no matter what challenges we're facing. Her stories are powerful, her approach is both biblical and practical, and her passion is contagious. More than once I wanted to jump to my feet and shout, 'Yes!' *Stand* has the power to change the church, one believer at a time. Put this book on your must-read list!"

Liz Curtis Higgs, bestselling author of *Bad Girls of the Bible*

"When the circumstances of life—or the pull of the world—threaten to topple you over, what will enable you to resist temptation and empower you to stand without wavering? Marian Jordan Ellis has penned an inspiring and spiritually helpful book full of scriptural examples and practical tools to help you form new thought patterns and position you to walk in victory. *Stand* will guide you through a process of honoring Christ as you overcome adversity by keeping your feet solidly planted in the word of God."

Karen Ehman, Proverbs 31 speaker and bestselling author of *Keep It Shut* and *Listen, Love, Repeat*

"Marian Jordan Ellis challenges readers to respond to trial and persecution in a powerfully counterintuitive way. *Stand* is a message of hope amidst hopelessness, faith amidst the fire, and light in the darkest of places."

Dr. Ben Young, teaching pastor at Second Baptist Church, Houston, TX

"Marian Jordan Ellis is a gifted writer and teacher. Honed by experience, she is able to convey biblical truths in relatable terms. Marian never leaves her reader hanging on a biblical principle without teaching the practical steps it takes to stand on that principle. This book will reach a wide audience ... both those who are mature in their faith and those who are seeking reasons to stand."

Dr. Ed Young, senior pastor, Second
Baptist Church, Houston, Texas

"In the challenging circumstances of life we need the power and perspective to stand in the midst of difficult days. In *Stand* Marian Jordan Ellis offers us a practical and faith-filled response to the biblical truth that our ultimate victory is in Jesus."

Ben Stuart, pastor of Passion City
Church, Washington, D.C.

"*Stand* is a vital message for the church today. Marian Jordan Ellis has equipped readers with powerful tools to resist temptation, overcome adversity, and believe God's promises in the midst of every trial. She beautifully draws from her own life and story and tethers her experience to the Word of God, which is able to withstand all heartbreak."

Tracy Wilde, author of *Finding the Lost Art of Empathy*

"This book will teach you how to conquer not only your emotional fears but also your spiritual fears. It will motivate you to stand and live a life full of faith in Jesus's strength. The words in this book are relevant and timely for every believer today."

Clayton and Sharie King, cofounders of Crossroads
Summer Camps and Clayton King Ministries

STAND

MARIAN JORDAN ELLIS

STAND

RISING UP AGAINST DARKNESS, TEMPTATION, AND PERSECUTION

David C Cook®
transforming lives together

STAND
Published by David C Cook
4050 Lee Vance Drive
Colorado Springs, CO 80918 U.S.A.

David C Cook U.K., Kingsway Communications
Eastbourne, East Sussex BN23 6NT, England

The graphic circle C logo is a registered trademark of David C Cook.

The website addresses recommended throughout this book are offered as a
resource to you. These websites are not intended in any way to be or imply an
endorsement on the part of David C Cook, nor do we vouch for their content.

The author has added italics to Scripture quotations for emphasis.

LCCN 2017931377
ISBN 978-0-7814-1497-5
eISBN 978-1-4347-1111-3

The Team: Tim Peterson, Keith Jones, Cara Iverson, Abby DeBenedittis,
Rachael Stevenson, Susan Murdock, Kayla Fenstermaker
Cover Design: Nick Lee

Printed in the United States of America
First Edition 2017

1 2 3 4 5 6 7 8 9 10

052517

To Andrew, Brenden, and Sydney.
I pray you always hold fast to the fact that Jesus wins
and stand firm in Him all the days of your lives.

CONTENTS

Introduction

· · · · · · · · ·

JESUS WINS

Stand firm, and you will win life.

Luke 21:19

Huddled around Jesus on the Mount of Olives, His disciples pressed close to hear Him relate the events that would occur before His victorious return at the end of the age. Like a quarterback calling the play, Jesus informed His ragtag team of followers what they should expect from their Enemy: wars, persecution, famine, hatred, ridicule, beatings, false accusations, temptation. Not exactly an encouraging list. Frankly, it sounds downright defeating. I can just imagine them giving one another a big-eyed stare as if to say, "Didn't we pick the winning team?"

Like the Twelve, most of us are not prepared for the difficult days when the Christian life feels as if there are just minutes remaining on the clock and we are ten points behind our opponent. I know I certainly wasn't. When I first surrendered my life to follow Christ,

I often heard promises of an abundant life, victory in Jesus, and blessings for obedience. Although all of these promises are true and proven in my life, what I didn't expect were days that would feel positively bleak and when victory seemed a distant hope.

I wasn't ready for the times when my faith would be tested or when I'd be forced to see past my present circumstances to the promises of God. No one prepared me for the season when my heart was broken in two and I felt abandoned by the Lord. I wasn't equipped for the battle against temptation that left me feeling overwhelmed. No one warned me about the days when I would see evil advance across the globe and question if God was working and moving. No one told me that despair could set in like fog. What I didn't know then but absolutely do know now is that these tests and trials are common. A spiritual battle between darkness and light is raging, and it can often feel as though darkness has the upper hand. We have a real Enemy, one who relishes the idea that we would feel defeated and walk away before we experience victory.

Trust me, I've felt the dismay the disciples must have experienced that night. I've felt the desire to walk off the field before the game is over. Having faced seasons of bewilderment, I understand why Jesus chose to warn us of the hardships that will come.

Jesus stepped onto the scene of human history to accomplish His Father's will to redeem and restore humanity to Himself. Every prophetic sign and messianic symbol were uniquely and perfectly fulfilled in the One who sat teaching His disciples on the Mount of Olives. As these men and women followed Him, they came to believe and hope that He was indeed the Promised One. As the Messiah, Jesus came with one purpose: to save those who put their hope in Him. And with His incarnation, the war that raged behind the scenes in the spiritual realm took center stage as He, the Light of the World, publicly displayed His dominion and authority over the kingdom of darkness. Defeating depravity, disease, demons, and death, Jesus demonstrated that He was (and is) truly the Son of God and the Savior.

Jesus accomplished His Father's will when He endured death on the cross, bearing our sins. Death could not hold Him, and three days later Jesus triumphed over it by rising from the grave. Today His victory is our victory. Although this is the best news of all time, the fact remains that we, His disciples, will face an ongoing battle against the kingdom of darkness until we see Him face-to-face. This battle is the reality Jesus prepared His disciples for as they sat with Him overlooking the city of Jerusalem.

> As Jesus was sitting on the Mount of Olives, the disciples came to him privately. "Tell us," they said, "when will this happen, and what will be the sign of your coming and of the end of the age?"
>
> Jesus answered: "Watch out that no one deceives you. For many will come in my name, claiming, 'I am the Messiah,' and will deceive many. You will hear of wars and rumors of wars, but see to it that you are not alarmed. Such things must happen, but the end is still to come. Nation will rise against nation, and kingdom against kingdom. There will be famines and earthquakes in various places. All these are the beginning of birth pains.

"Then you will be handed over to be persecuted
and put to death, and you will be hated by all nations
because of me. At that time many will turn away
from the faith and will betray and hate each other,
and many false prophets will appear and deceive
many people. Because of the increase of wickedness,
the love of most will grow cold, *but the one who
stands firm to the end will be saved.*" (Matt. 24:3–13)

Keep in mind that these disciples abandoned everything to follow Jesus. They left their homes, careers, and possessions to follow
the One they believed was the Savior of the world. Fixing their hope
on this rabbi from Nazareth as the long-awaited Messiah, they went
all in. These twelve men expected victory and hoped in Christ for
deliverance from the Enemy. But then this same Jesus began to tell
them of dark days to come—trials, hardships, persecutions, wars,
famines, earthquakes, and global turmoil—before His return.

In the midst of His clear warning and instructions, Jesus sensed
the disciples' fears and knew precisely what was at stake. That's one
reason He gave them this beautiful promise of victory: "Stand firm,
and you will win life" (Luke 21:19). Although it may feel as if the
Enemy has the upper hand and though the scoreboard doesn't always
seem in our favor, Jesus essentially says, "I've got this." Don't judge
by what you perceive with your physical eyes. See with eyes of faith.
If you stand, you will win.

To the disciples, who were trying to reconcile Jesus's words with
their own expectations, He went on to promise the greatest victory of
all time. The saying "It's always darkest before the dawn" applies here.

Jesus pointed them forward to when He will triumphantly return to redeem, restore, and rectify all things. Speaking of His triumphant second coming, He told us, "They will see the Son of Man coming in a cloud with power and great glory. When these things begin to take place, stand up and lift up your heads, because your redemption is drawing near" (Luke 21:27–28).

I absolutely love this call: "Stand up and lift up your heads, because your redemption is drawing near." Jesus said to take this stance because it is when we feel defeated that our heads drop and shoulders slump as we give in to the voices of doom and depression. If you've ever watched the finals of a championship game, you've seen this posture. Without even knowing the score, I can always tell by the physical posture of the fans which team is winning. The fans expecting victory are standing tall, leaning in, with their heads lifted high and their eyes full of expectation. The ones expecting defeat are slumped over in despair or making their way toward the exit. Jesus reminded us that the clock hasn't run out. He will return in glory, and He will bring the ultimate victory over darkness that we long to see. Therefore, we are to keep our heads held high and stand firm till the end.

WHY STAND?

Stand. If you think about it, you'll see that it is a peculiar word for Jesus to give His disciples. Continuing our sports metaphor, we can imagine a coach telling the team to train hard for an upcoming battle, run faster than the opponents, or build up a better defense. Jesus didn't give any of these commands. He simply said for us to *stand.* The reason for this unexpected call is that victory is not found in our efforts, ability, or skill. Instead, it's found solely in the power and authority of our great God. We stand, unmoved and unshaken, steadfast in faith, with our hope fixed on the promises of God and His power to deliver.

The call to stand is a call to faith. It means to hold fast to our God-confidence and not lose ground. It is the call to rise up against the forces that oppose us and hold our position of victory instead of cowering in defeat. For the Christ follower, the call to stand speaks of our posture of faith in the midst of trials, our position of victory during an attack, our power in Christ to overcome, and our perseverance to the end.

The ones who stand are the people who keep hope alive, don't give up, and refuse to back down. Their bold confidence is rooted in the fact that darkness will not prevail, because Jesus is victorious. The ones who stand look into the face of the fiercest opponent or obstacle and rejoice with hope because they know, deep within their hearts, that the scoreboard doesn't determine destiny. These men and women, young and old, are what Scripture calls *overcomers*. Sure, the Enemy deals out trials and temptations, but the ones who stand firm are the ones who choose to trust Jesus and believe, even in the darkest night, that Jesus wins!

Standing means watching with eyes of faith until we see the victory. When we heed the call to stand, Jesus gives us a powerful promise: "You will win life" (Luke 21:19).

Jesus promises us:

- Our darkest days are not our destiny.
- The Enemy's fiercest attacks are not our identity.
- The evil of this present world is not our future reality.

God's Word is filled with specific promises to those who stand—promises of blessings, eternal rewards, and everlasting life. Jesus summed up the promises with these words: "You will win life." The battles we face are not in vain. Our fight to overcome sin is not futile. The struggle to hold fast to faith in the midst of trials is not pointless, because great honor and blessings await those who stand firm.

I don't know about you, but I need this word of encouragement. From watching persecution increase across the globe to seeing Christians falling into sin at unprecedented rates, I can't turn on the television or tune into social media without seeing the church (in all its forms) taking a serious beating. In the past few years, I've felt that darkness has not only increased but also seems to be winning. Christian values are mocked, and those who hold them are maligned.

When I look at the world with my natural eyes, it's easy to cave in to fear and feel discouraged, lose hope, and question the promises of God. It seems as though Christ followers are down for the count and the Enemy is doing a victory dance in the end zone. Call me competitive, but I don't relish the idea of being on the losing end of anything. When I see depravity escalating or suffering mounting, I find myself, much like the disciples, wide-eyed and wondering what Jesus is up to. At those times, when I'm tempted to wave the white flag and just call it a day, I find myself fighting for hope.

Hope. What a beautiful word and desperately needed reality for Christ followers. Hope moves beyond intellectual belief. It's supernatural faith that takes spiritually weak muscles paralyzed with fear and doubt and gives them the miraculous ability to stand. Hope perseveres even when it seems that all is lost in the natural realm.

Here's the thing: I know the end of the story. Our Enemy is defeated and Jesus wins. The Bible is crystal clear on this fact. But on those dark days, when it seems like we're on the losing team, I find myself asking, "What do we do, Lord?" Turning to His Word, I discover the answer: we stand.

Please hear me: this isn't a simple Christian cliché worthy of bumper-sticker status. Jesus gave us the word *stand* as an answer to our struggles, fears, and battles. How do we as Christ followers press on toward victory in this age of rampant temptations, persecutions, and accusations? How do we remain steadfast when our hearts are broken wide open with grief and the Enemy chooses those moments to mock our faith in God? How do we respond when we are called names for our biblical convictions? How do we react to the injustices we see in the world? How do we resist the pressure to conform morally? How do we get back up when we've fallen?

We stand.

As I survey my friends and family, I see similar questions:

- How does one stand firm in faith, hoping in God in the midst of heartbreak and unmet desires?
- How do Christian leaders share the gospel in a culture that wants to silence us?
- How does the Christian executive stand in the face of shady business dealings?
- How does one hold fast to truth in an age of relativity and false teaching?

- How do parents stand in hope when their children are more in love with the world than they are with Jesus?
- How does a Christian battle the voices of shame and insecurity?
- How does one stand against the pull of pornography?
- How does one believe victory is accomplished when it feels as though darkness is winning?

Throughout Scripture, the word *stand* is repeated over and over to the people of faith. It is our posture in the face of temptation, persecution, suffering, and doubt. I think that because repetition is the key to learning, God is trying to teach us something. Just take a look at these examples:

> Moses answered the people, "Do not be afraid. *Stand firm* and you will see the deliverance the LORD will bring you today. The Egyptians you see today you will never see again. (Exod. 14:13)

> [God told King Jehoshaphat:] "You will not have to fight this battle. Take up your positions; *stand firm* and see the deliverance the LORD will give you, Judah and Jerusalem. Do not be afraid; do not be discouraged. Go out to face them tomorrow, and the LORD will be with you." (2 Chron. 20:17)

[Jesus said:] "You will be hated by everyone because of me, but the one who *stands firm* to the end will be saved." (Matt. 10:22)

Be strong in the Lord and in his mighty power. Put on the full armor of God, so that you can take your *stand* against the devil's schemes. For our struggle is not against flesh and blood, but against the rulers, against the authorities, against the powers of this dark world and against the spiritual forces of evil in the heavenly realms. (Eph. 6:10–12)

If you think you are *standing firm*, be careful that you don't fall! No temptation has overtaken you except what is common to mankind. And God is faithful; he will not let you be tempted beyond what you can bear. But when you are tempted, he will also provide a way out so that you can endure it. (1 Cor. 10:12–13)

As I survey these passages of Scripture, I see a theme. The Lord prepares us for battle. He shoots straight with us, letting us know there will be tough times but reminding us that our call in the midst of the Enemy's schemes, temptations, trials, and persecutions is to stand and see the deliverance of the Lord!

We hear the word *stand* and often think of Christians taking a stand *against* something. I don't believe that is exactly what Jesus meant when He said, "Stand firm, and you will win life." I'm pretty confident

stand firm
not
stand against

He didn't envision some social-media rant or physical confrontation at a retail store. Standing is not about being against someone else; it's about being found in Jesus Christ, who is our victory.

To stand means to remain faithful, endure till the end, hold fast, and persevere when hope wanes and evil confronts. This call is for us to fix our eyes on Jesus and believe that He will accomplish what He's promised. *Stand* is the resolve to believe God even when fear or other feelings suggest otherwise.

STAND OR BOW?

As Christ followers, we face a culture hostile to our beliefs and faith. We live in a world in which our values are not held by society at large. What will we do when the heat turns up and we face a decision to stand in faith or bow down to relational, social, economic, or governmental pressures? Jesus warned us to expect persecution and temptation to conform both morally and spiritually. But for most of us, that warning seemed far in the distance. Now that warning looms before us as a reality. Thankfully, Jesus prepared us for these times and promised us victory.

The question before us is this: Will we stand?

I know of no better example in God's Word of a choice to stand in the midst of a culture opposed to Christ than the story of Shadrach, Meshach, and Abednego found in the book of Daniel. Three men embodied the call to stand and teach us in a powerful way what it looks like to "win life."

Context is extremely important here. God's people were captives in Babylon, an empire hostile to the Lord's ways. While exiled there, the king of Babylon pronounced a decree that all people were to bow down and worship a golden statue dedicated to himself. The problem with this command is that it violated the biblical call to "serve [the Lord] *only*" (Deut. 6:13). Shadrach, Meshach, and Abednego faced a clear choice: Would they fall down and worship with the crowds around them or stand and face the consequences?

The satraps, prefects, governors, advisers, treasurers, judges, magistrates and all the other provincial officials assembled for the dedication of the image that King Nebuchadnezzar had set up, and they stood before it.

Then the herald loudly proclaimed, "Nations and peoples of every language, this is what you are commanded to do: As soon as you hear the sound of the horn, flute, zither, lyre, harp, pipe and all kinds of music, you must fall down and worship the image of gold that King Nebuchadnezzar has set up. Whoever does not fall down and worship will immediately be thrown into a blazing furnace."

Therefore, as soon as they heard the sound of the horn, flute, zither, lyre, harp and all kinds of music, all the nations and peoples of every language fell down and worshiped the image of gold that King Nebuchadnezzar had set up.

At this time some astrologers came forward and denounced the Jews. They said to King Nebuchadnezzar, "May the king live forever! Your

Majesty has issued a decree that everyone who hears
the sound of the horn, flute, zither, lyre, harp, pipe
and all kinds of music must fall down and worship
the image of gold, and that whoever does not fall
down and worship will be thrown into a blazing furnace. But there are some Jews whom you have set over
the affairs of the province of Babylon—Shadrach,
Meshach and Abednego—who pay no attention to
you, Your Majesty. They neither serve your gods nor
worship the image of gold you have set up."

Furious with rage, Nebuchadnezzar summoned
Shadrach, Meshach and Abednego. So these men
were brought before the king, and Nebuchadnezzar
said to them, "Is it true, Shadrach, Meshach and
Abednego, that you do not serve my gods or worship the image of gold I have set up? Now when you
hear the sound of the horn, flute, zither, lyre, harp,
pipe and all kinds of music, if you are ready to fall
down and worship the image I made, very good.
But if you do not worship it, you will be thrown
immediately into a blazing furnace. Then what god
will be able to rescue you from my hand?"

Shadrach, Meshach and Abednego replied to
him, "King Nebuchadnezzar, we do not need to
defend ourselves before you in this matter. If we are
thrown into the blazing furnace, *the God we serve
is able to deliver us* from it, and he will deliver us
from Your Majesty's hand. *But even if he does not,*

we want you to know, Your Majesty, that *we will not serve your gods or worship the image of gold you have set up.*" (Dan. 3:3–18)

Oh, how I wish I were standing before you with my Bible in hand, teaching this amazing passage of Scripture! I would do what my friends lovingly call the "holy hop." You see, when I get super excited about God's Word, I tend to jump up and down a tiny bit. Wow! Reading the bold response of these three men astounds and inspires me. Their resolve in the face of unbelievable pressure portrays for us the unwavering posture of one who stands.

Just think about it: three normal guys looked the most powerful man in the world in the eyes and said, "We will not bow down" (v. 18 GNT). They calculated the risk and considered the Lord worth it. Their choice to stand was based on two truths: they believed that God was more than able to deliver them from their enemy, and they believed the Lord's glory was worthy of their stance.

In the course of life, all Christ followers will face this same choice. As darkness increases around us, the pressure to conform and go along with the crowd will grow and grow. Therefore, we must build up our faith muscles so we can stand firm when the pressure is most intense. As we will see in the second half of Shadrach, Meshach, and Abednego's story, due to their unwavering faith and fearless resolve, the king of Babylon became an eyewitness to their deliverance and ultimately glorified God.

Then Nebuchadnezzar was furious with Shadrach, Meshach and Abednego, and his attitude toward them changed. He ordered the furnace heated seven times hotter than usual and commanded some of the strongest soldiers in his army to tie up Shadrach, Meshach and Abednego and throw them into the blazing furnace. So these men, wearing their robes, trousers, turbans and other clothes, were bound and thrown into the blazing furnace. The king's command was so urgent and the furnace so hot that the flames of the fire killed the soldiers who took up Shadrach, Meshach and Abednego, and these three men, firmly tied, fell into the blazing furnace.

Then King Nebuchadnezzar leaped to his feet in amazement and asked his advisers, "Weren't there three men that we tied up and threw into the fire?"

They replied, "Certainly, Your Majesty."

He said, "Look! I see four men walking around in the fire, unbound and unharmed, and the fourth looks like a son of the gods."

Nebuchadnezzar then approached the opening of the blazing furnace and shouted, "Shadrach, Meshach and Abednego, servants of the Most High God, come out! Come here!"

So Shadrach, Meshach and Abednego came out of the fire, and the satraps, prefects, governors and royal advisers crowded around them. They saw that the fire had not harmed their bodies, nor was a hair of their heads singed; their robes were not scorched, and there was no smell of fire on them.

Then Nebuchadnezzar said, "Praise be to the God
of Shadrach, Meshach and Abednego, who has sent
his angel and rescued his servants! They trusted in him
and defied the king's command and were willing to
give up their lives rather than serve or worship any
god except their own God. Therefore I decree that the
people of any nation or language who say anything
against the God of Shadrach, Meshach and Abednego
be cut into pieces and their houses be turned into piles
of rubble, for no other god can save in this way."

Then the king promoted Shadrach, Meshach and
Abednego in the province of Babylon. (vv. 19–30)

Yes, Shadrach, Meshach, and Abednego faced the fiery furnace
because they chose to stand, but the earth-shaking, king-quaking,
life-altering truth is this: the Lord God Almighty stood with them in
the midst of the fire! They were not alone, and they were delivered
from the furnace without even smelling like smoke!

These three men served as living examples of what Christ meant
when He said, "Stand firm, and you will win life." In the midst of
intense temptation to conform and internal pressure to save their
own necks, they resolved not to bow down and chose instead to plant
their feet on the faithfulness of God. And, wow, did they win life!
The Lord displayed His glory in their lives in such a powerful way.
As a result of their fearless faith, the most powerful man at the time
worshipped the Lord.

Friends, this book is not about external hot-button issues; it
is about the internal resolve of the committed Christian to remain

faithful to God until the end. The external issues we face will change. As a student of church history, I can tell you one thing: there is nothing new under the sun. Christians in every generation have needed to stand against evil, oppression, temptation, and persecution. The fallen world will always be the fallen world. Darkness will always be dark, and the church is always expected to be light, and the battle between the two is a given. As believers, the pressures we face to blend in will shift over time, but the internal resolve to choose Christ must be within us before we can meet the challenges before us.

In this book, we will examine in Scripture what it means to "stand firm, and ... win life."

Stand is divided into four sections. Each section empowers us to stand firm in different seasons and equips us with truth to overcome.

Part 1: The Posture of Faith. In these chapters, we journey back to Exodus and learn from Moses how to stand and see God's deliverance in the midst of our biggest faith-testing moments. As our faith muscles grow and our relationships with God deepen, so does our ability to stand firm against the pressures of this world.

Part 2: The Planted Feet. In this section, we dive into God's Word and learn how to stand firmly on the Solid Rock (Jesus Christ) and realize the blessing of building our lives upon His truth. In order to hold our ground against spiritual warfare, persecution, and temptation, we must first know who we are as beloved children of God.

Part 3: The Position of Victory. Next we will turn our attention to spiritual warfare. The call to stand against the forces of darkness is repeated throughout the New Testament. In these chapters, we will learn from the apostle Paul how to take up the full armor of God and stand in the victory that is ours in Jesus Christ.

Part 4: The Promise to Overcomers. Throughout God's Word, those who stand firm until the end are called overcomers. In this final section, we will learn how to rise up against persecution and discover the rewards awaiting those who overcome.

Each section of this book equips us for the next. Without a firm faith and solid understanding of the gospel, we aren't equipped to resist the Enemy in times of spiritual warfare or persecution. Throughout this book, we will also take a close look at real people, people who, when faced with dark days, believed God and remained steadfast. This journey will take us all over God's Word. We will hear the call to stand and learn to plant our feet firmly in the person and promises of God.

YOU MAY BE DOWN, BUT YOU CAN STAND

One of the all-time greatest Olympic moments was when US gymnast Kerri Strug made her heroic comeback. If you aren't old enough to remember, I highly recommend that you watch the clip on YouTube. Oh, and don't forget to bring tissues. It's a tearjerker.

Strug was a member of the 1996 US women's gymnastics team. She was not the golden girl, not by a long shot. She stood in the shadows of the all-stars. To add even more pressure, Team USA had never won a team gold medal, and expectations were high for victory.

The team faced a fierce battle with the Russians for gold. But with a significant lead, they entered the final competition: the vault. Most assumed the Americans had victory in the bag, until, shockingly, Team USA's lead began to evaporate after Dominique Moceanu, one of the stars, fell not once but twice, leaving gold in jeopardy.

All hope of victory now came down to Kerri Strug. With the crowd on its feet, she took a deep breath and sprinted down the seventy-five-foot runway, performing a vault she'd practiced more than a thousand times. After descending through the air toward the ground, she slipped on her landing, felt a snap in her left ankle, and fell onto the mat.

Disbelief filled the gymnasium. When Strug's score—9.162—flashed on the board, it appeared the gold was gone.

Turmoil hit Team USA.

Should she try again? Should she sit it out? Is the hope of victory lost?

Strug's ankle throbbed badly. She was in tremendous pain and felt the heavy weight of disappointment on her shoulders.

Then her coach, Béla Károlyi, walked over to her, put his arm around her, and said, "Kerri, we need you to go one more time. We need you one more time for the gold."[1]

In an unbelievable act of courage and resolve, Strug rose from the floor, removed the ice pack from her ankle, and prayed, "Please, God, help me make this vault."[2]

Strug sprints down the runway on her damaged ankle. Across the way, the Russian gymnasts … stop and watch. Strug leaps high into the air. She performs a back handspring onto the vault, perfectly. Then she descends through the air, toward the ground. Everyone on the sidelines and in the crowd winces, knowing that when Strug lands, it's going to be as painful as someone smashing a [metal] rod against your ankle.

Strug lands hard on both feet, amazingly without stumbling. Yet when she lands, she hears another crack in the same ankle. She gingerly picks up her damaged ankle and folds it behind her, keeping her balance, to the shock of everyone in the crowd and everyone watching on TV. *Her mind tells her body to stand* upright for the traditional post-performance pose. She hops on one foot to face one side of the crowd, then hops again to face the other, all the while holding up her injured ankle.

Strug's teammates begin leaping on the sideline. Strug, meanwhile, hops around a quarter turn, arms raised, and forces a big smile for the judges while the Georgia Dome crowd of 32,048 lets out a roar.[3] (emphasis added)

Please don't miss this line: "Her mind tells her body to stand." Just as Kerri Strug needed to find the inner resolve to get off the mat, so do we. There comes a point in each of our journeys that we must make the choice to stand. Kerri Strug was down, the gold was as good as gone, yet somewhere inside this tiny gymnast was the resolve of a giant. Facing an incredible obstacle, she overcame and planted her landing, standing firm and winning Olympic gold.

- Standing firm is a choice.
- Standing firm is getting back up when life knocks you down.
- Standing firm is overcoming the voice of defeat and believing that victory is won.

Perhaps you're reading this right now and you too are down on the mat. Maybe you've been dealt a hand of heartache that has you doubled over in grief. Or perhaps you've succumbed to a temptation that you never thought you'd fall for and you're now in the clutches of sin. Perhaps you are feeling worldly pressures to silence your voice and commitment to Jesus. Wherever you are on your journey, I want to encourage you. Your darkest moment isn't your destiny. You may be down on the mat today, but you can rise, and you can stand! You can experience incredible victory and live a life that glorifies God.

Friend, this book is for you.

> Do not rejoice over me, my enemy!
> Though I have fallen, I will stand up;
> though I sit in darkness,
> the LORD will be my light. (Mic. 7:8 HCSB)

STAND

· · · · · · · · · · ·

THE POSTURE OF FAITH

Be on your guard; stand firm in the faith; be courageous; be strong.

1 Corinthians 16:13

Chapter 1

· · · · · · ·

STAND AND SEE

Moses answered the people, "Do not be afraid. Stand firm and
you will see the deliverance the LORD *will bring you today.*
The Egyptians you see today you will never see again.

Exodus 14:13

If you've ever been crushed by heartache, disappointment, or grief
or known the deep ache of an unmet desire, then you know that the
first thing your body wants to do in these moments is crumple to the
ground in defeat. This physical posture mirrors what occurs in our
souls. During seasons of suffering, we are severely tempted to lose hope,
give up on God, and believe that Jesus has forsaken us. It is in these
times of testing that we must rise up, put feet to our faith, and stand.

The call to stand firm in these difficult moments is not easy, but
when we do, God shows off. His glorious power, plan, and purpose
are revealed in our moments of profound weakness.

Here is my story.

BLINDSIDED

The man I loved walked out the door with no promise to return. As I watched him walk to his car, I could barely move from the place where my feet were planted. Cemented to the spot where my heart bled, I mustered the strength to pray, "Jesus, help me."

Justin walked away with my heart and my hope for our future. Every cell in my body screamed a protest, and I wanted more than anything to cave in to self-pity and shake my fist at God in objection. But something happened in my heart: I sensed the Lord whisper, "Marian, stand."

Before that fateful night, ours was a storybook romance. We met, fell in love, and I just knew. It was like in the movies—only this one was pure and lovely, like a Jane Austen film. Justin was my person, my best friend, and he loved Jesus more than anyone I had ever known. Oh, and bonus: he was taller than me! For this five-foot-eleven girl, that fact was a miracle.

Let's just say I was giddy.

You should know a little of my backstory. I was in my late thirties when I met him. I was single and had waited far longer than I ever expected for God to provide the desires of my heart. I was the old cliché: always the bridesmaid but never the bride. Anyone who's walked through an unmet desire of any kind knows the pain that accompanies emptiness. Through that season of waiting, there were many moments of grief and I fought hard to believe in the goodness of God in the midst of my unmet desire. But then one crazy, awkward day in February, when I was least expecting to fall in love, I went on a blind date with the man who stole my heart.

As spring rolled into summer and summer into fall, friends and family gave their hearty approval of the match. Therefore, I began to let down my walls and hope and plan for the future. But then, out of the blue, the man I loved went through a rough patch. Looking back now, I know it was spiritual warfare (more on that in upcoming chapters), but at the time, it felt as though a cloud of fear, darkness, and doubt had descended upon our relationship. Justin was in a battle that I couldn't really understand or fix.

Around the time that I was expecting a proposal, he told me in no uncertain terms that he couldn't move forward in our relationship. He didn't want to hurt me, but he couldn't overcome the fear and doubt hammering against his chest. He needed to end it. Two small little letters, but that simple *it* was our relationship, our future, our potential marriage.

To say I was shocked by the turn of events is an understatement. Everything had seemed perfect, until the cloud descended upon him like nothing I've ever seen. Sure, I knew he was struggling, but I didn't think it would come to this.

At first I began to offer words of encouragement and tell him why it would be okay, but then I sensed God telling me to stop. In my heart, I heard the call to stand. I sensed the Lord wanted me to trust Him, take my hands off the situation, and let Him work.

If you've ever been through a heartbreak of any kind, you know from experience what the Enemy loves to do in those moments. He loves to speak fear and doubt in our ears. To keep us from walking by faith, he seeks opportunities to lie to us about God's character. We are most vulnerable to spiritual attack during those seasons. In many ways, pain proves an open door for the Adversary to breathe lies. Fear says that trusting God with our desires is foolish. Doubt says the Lord can't fix the situation, so *we* had better take control. Yet in that moment, the Lord called me to walk by faith. He asked me to trust Him with my heart and entrust the "fixing" of Justin to Him.

To trust God with my heart proved a test. Before I met Justin and fell in love with him, I had already walked through a painful heartbreak and experienced the crushing blow of rejection. Then I waited a very long time to meet the one I believed was my future husband and fall in love. Now that "love" was walking out the door.

Could I trust God with this relationship? Furthermore, could I trust God with my heart?

Much to my surprise, I heeded the call. I didn't put up a fight; I let Justin leave. Without a word, I let him go.

With his exit, I let go of a relationship that was sweeter than anything I could have imagined. I let go of my dream of our future together. I let go of any control over his decisions or what might happen the next day or the days after. God was calling me to see how He would work without my help, and every human instinct screamed for me to do the opposite. I wanted to stage a confrontation in the front yard and convince him that his fears were unfounded and that we could overcome this. Instead, I simply let go.

I felt as if I were facing my biggest fear. I also felt helpless to do anything to change my situation. Just as the waves of self-pity, rejection, and deep sadness began to mount, I sensed the Lord speak clear words to my heart: "Marian, stand."

MORE THAN WE CAN HANDLE

There's an old saying I hear from time to time that just burns my biscuits: "God will never give you more than you can handle." I find this cliché complete garbage. For starters, we can't find this idea anywhere in Scripture. I'm sure King David, the apostle Paul, and every saint in between would laugh at the mere suggestion. All of them faced scenarios that were far more than they could handle. They not only needed but also required divine power and God's grace to withstand the Enemy and overcome trials.

Just imagine King David running toward Goliath and yelling back to his brothers, "Don't worry, I've got this!" Of course, that's not how the famous Bible story went down. Instead, the young shepherd boy charged out toward him, boasting solely in the greatness and power of his God. It was in the Lord's ability that David found the courage to overcome his weakness and slay the giant before him. David was humble enough to realize that Goliath was more than he could handle but was nothing compared to his God. It was young David's confidence in the Lord that emboldened him to prevail in battle. Sure, we all face problems, people, and pitfalls that prove more than we can handle, but nothing we face is ever more than *He* can handle.

In addition, this belief that God will never give us more than we can handle goes against the realities of the Christian life. Jesus prepared us to expect dark days when our faith would be tested and seasons in which we would be called to stand firm against darkness. We are called to stand because in these times of profound weakness, we see and experience God's tremendous power on our behalf. In the moments that are "more than we can handle," we discover the greatness of our God.

- When your relationships are more than you can handle, stand and see.
- When your finances are more than you can handle, stand and see.
- When your children are more than you can handle, stand and see.
- When your emotions are more than you can handle, stand and see.
- When your broken heart is more than you can handle, stand and see.

It's okay if you feel as though your current situation is more than you can handle. That's where you can experience God's greatest strength. You may be at the end of yourself, and that's okay because in our weakness He is strong.

When we find ourselves with our backs against the wall, our prayers are fueled by desperation and our faith is zeroed in on the only One who can remedy our situations. In seasons of life that are more than we can handle, we experience God's power and presence profoundly. In these tests, we learn to stand. Here's how the apostle Paul expressed this reality:

> [The Lord] said to me, "My grace is sufficient for you, for my power is made perfect in weakness." Therefore I will boast all the more gladly about my

weaknesses, so that Christ's power may rest on me. That is why, for Christ's sake, I delight in weaknesses, in insults, in hardships, in persecutions, in difficulties. For when I am weak, then I am strong. (2 Cor. 12:9–11)

We can't handle life on our own, and frankly, I don't think we are meant to try. In the midst of our profound weakness, we discover God's great strength.

Throughout this chapter and the next two, we will take an up-close look at Moses and the children of Israel as they face a scenario far greater than anyone could handle. This crisis of faith, which we will call a Red Sea moment, will become the primary example for us of standing firm in the midst of the trials and temptations of this world. Just as Moses stood firm before Pharaoh with an unwavering belief in the power and presence of God, so will we learn to stand firm before the Enemy in the victory of Christ.

Just as Jesus promised us that we would "win life" if we hold our ground, so we see in this Exodus story that great blessings hinged on whether Moses and God's people would stand firm by trusting the Lord, overcoming their fears, and holding their ground against their enemy.

The Lord's purpose in delivering the children of Israel out of slavery in Egypt was to take them into the land of their inheritance: the Promised Land. It has this name because this is where the people of God would see His covenant promises fulfilled and where they would claim their spiritual inheritance. In order to get there, they first faced a daunting test and a ruthless enemy.

Journey back in time with me to the land of Egypt. Imagine Moses leading the Israelites from slavery in Egypt to freedom in the Promised Land. There, on the shore of the Red Sea, we observe one of the greatest showdowns in the history of the world and discover the power of faith to stand firm and win life! Moses provides a vivid illustration of faith that stands firm, and the story is the source of what the Lord said to me the fateful night I faced my own Red Sea moment.

RED SEA MOMENTS

Hoofbeats pounded thunderously in the distance, and chariot wheels squealed as Pharaoh's army closed in on the Israelites at the edge of the Red Sea. Panic gripped the masses surrounding Moses when they saw their former captors drawing near. Pandemonium ensued as the Egyptian army grew closer and Israel's hope of freedom seemed to blow away in the desert wind. As he stoof firm in the midst of this chaos, a supernatural calm covered Moses. He was not swept up in the frenzy of fear like others around him; instead, he fixed his eyes upon the great I AM. Enveloped in the majesty and power of the Almighty, Moses chose to stand.

> As Pharaoh approached, the Israelites looked up, and there were the Egyptians, marching after them. They were terrified and cried out to the LORD. They said to Moses, "Was it because there were no graves in Egypt that you brought us to the desert to die? What have you done to us by bringing us out of

Egypt? Didn't we say to you in Egypt, 'Leave us alone; let us serve the Egyptians'? It would have been better for us to serve the Egyptians than to die in the desert!"

Moses answered the people, "Do not be afraid. *Stand firm and you will see the deliverance the LORD will bring you today.* The Egyptians you see today you will never see again. The LORD will fight for you; you need only to be still." (Exod. 14:10–14)

Slip on Moses's sandals for a moment. What would you have done with an army behind you, a sea before you, and nowhere to hide? Would you have dug a hole in the sand to hide or thrown yourself into the sea to swim for safety? When faced with threats or fears, most of us are hardwired to choose between two things: fight or flight. But there is a supernatural third option for the faithful.

Although the vast majority of us will never find ourselves with an army breathing down our backs and certain death before us, we will surely face scenarios where our faith is put to the test. I know I've experienced my own Red Sea moments: those times when everything in the natural realm told me to doubt God, when I was tempted to take matters into my hands, or when I caved in to ungodly emotions. Whether it is a season of unemployment or a family relationship in shambles or an unexpected health crisis, there will be points in our journeys with God when He calls us to stand and see.

To stand is to put feet to our faith. This is far more than an intellectual set of beliefs; this is a confidence in the Lord that overrides all voices of fear. It means trusting in God even when our circumstances scream for us to do otherwise. These Red Sea moments are when all our Bible studies, Scripture memorization, and singing of worship songs must be more than just words. At the Red Sea, faith is no longer a theory but a living, breathing reality.

From the couple struggling with infertility to the Christian businessperson belittled for holding to biblical values to the single person beset with loneliness to the couple fighting for their marriage, there will be days when we feel backed into a corner and desperate for deliverance. For some of you, it may come in the form of waves of doubt crashing against you or persecution tempting you to buckle your knees. But these are the moments that require us to stand. They are varied and unique to our stories, but the one thing consistent in each of our experiences is that faith is a choice.

In our Red Sea moments, we must take what we know about God and stand upon His truths. To believe God even when facing heartbreak, to obey God even when the world mocks our values, to maintain peace in the midst of a storm—that is what it means to stand.

That split second when Moses believed God and chose to stand changed the destiny of an entire nation. He could have bowed down to Pharaoh, begged for mercy, or run in fear, but he chose to stand. That was the moment that made the man. He planted his feet on the promises of God, fixed his gaze on the presence of the Lord, and adjusted his physical posture to reflect the faith of his heart.

Standing doesn't mean we are free from the presence of fear. Instead, it means we choose to trust God in the midst of it.

I can't write these words without thinking of my friend Kathy. Three years ago, she sat in a doctor's office and was handed a death sentence. The medical community declared her cancer beyond hope of human intervention. She was too far gone, they said. They gave her only a few weeks to live. Like Moses, every possible emotion hit her like a tidal wave. That's only natural. But deeper still, where the waves of fear couldn't reach, lay a bedrock of faith that overcame the onslaught.

Three years later, she defied the odds and astounded the physicians. Was she healed? No. But she chose to stand and fight. Kathy stood firm in her faith through the pain, sickness, grief, and sinister attacks from the Enemy. She trusted the Lord daily with her life and with the lives of her young children. She chose to hope in Him even though she could not see the future.

Kathy stood firm in the face of cancer and ultimately death itself. Just last week, she slipped into the arms of Jesus. Through it all, she held fast to her faith and looked forward each day, with joy, to her heavenly home. Throughout it all, she held her ground against an Enemy who wanted to steal her confidence, joy, and peace. She taught her children and thousands of us who witnessed her unwavering resolve to believe God.

Her resolve was rooted in the power, presence, and promises of God. Although she couldn't see the future, she chose to trust the One who can. Although she couldn't see heaven with her physical eyes, she chose to trust the One who defeated death on the cross and promised to make all things new. Kathy believed that God could turn all things, even cancer, into something glorious.

I believe that this same courage and resolve to trust God rose up in Moses when he faced his own impossible situation.

From the widespread panic gripping the Israelites to the furious pursuit of Pharaoh's army, this showdown at the Red Sea appeared from an onlooker's perspective to be the perfect storm of chaos and fear. Yet on the inside, Moses experienced peace that surpassed understanding as he trusted in the presence, power, and promises of God.

Pastor and author Steven Furtick wrote, "Our faith may fail. But God's faithfulness never will. Our faith is not built on the fault line of feelings or the flood plain of our performance. We build our faith on solid ground. Higher ground. We build on the faithfulness of God."[1] This is the type of unwavering faith we see in Moses. He believed God. He believed that God's past faithfulness was an indicator of His future performance.

When Moses arrived at a place that seemed to be certain death, he chose to see his circumstances through eyes of faith. Therefore, with bold confidence, Moses said to the people, "Do not be afraid. Stand firm and you will see the deliverance the LORD will bring you today. The Egyptians you see today you will never see again" (Exod. 14:13).

With Pharaoh's army fast approaching, Moses found himself and the people completely surrounded. Out-armed, overpowered, and with the Red Sea before them, mountains surrounding them, and an army pursuing them, they were trapped. Moses couldn't run (not with more than two million people in tow), and he sure couldn't hide.

This was more than Moses could handle. He had two choices: trust God or fear Pharaoh.

JULIE'S RED SEA MOMENT

My friend Julie faced her own Red Sea moment, one that proved to be more than she could handle. Today she testifies to the Lord's deliverance when she faced down her greatest fear.

> I grew up in a beautiful southern state. From the outside, my childhood looked like everyone else's in the Bible Belt. I was taught to love God and be a good girl. We were religious people, yet a secret shame existed at home: sexual perversions and abuse were rampant. It seemed to follow us for generations, and I was just one more victim.
>
> Fast-forward to when I became a mother. Jesus had redeemed and healed my life from the sin committed against me and from my rebellious choices. I wanted a far different life for my kids. I prayed this sin would end with me and wouldn't touch my children. My husband and I read parenting books, taught our kids the Word, and faithfully served in our church. I did all the "right" things. I was vigilant about protecting them and watched over them like a hawk. As hard as I tried, I couldn't protect my kids from Satan's schemes.
>
> When our son was twelve years old, we discovered pornographic material on his iPad. I was physically sickened by the discovery. I cried hot tears and felt punched in the gut. But more than that, I

felt betrayed. How could God allow this when we did all the right things?

I thought that if I followed the rules, I could prevent this evil from reaching my doorstep. I thought that in the Lord's sovereignty He could have stopped this darkness from touching my kid, but He didn't. I couldn't wrap my mind around this disappointment.

We waited a few days before talking to our son about the pornography. During that time, I wrestled with God about my hurt and anxiety, letting out all my raw feelings that I didn't need to dump on a twelve-year-old. He was too young to process my painful history and how much I feared his repeating my story.

I heard the Lord say, *The absence of evil won't change the legacy of your family. It is how you handle your son in the presence of this darkness that will change his destiny. I can restore your son; you need to entrust him to Me.*

This was my Red Sea moment. Could I trust God as I locked eyes with the Enemy? Fear screamed in my ears, "No!" Every monstrous outcome that swarmed my mind wanted me to doubt God's goodness and take back control.

I realized there were two drastically different responses I could have: one was to react in fear, and the other was to stand in faith. Fear looked at the Enemy's agenda and felt defeated. Fear wanted me to control my kid, belittle and shame him for his sin, and micromanage his every waking move. But faith called me to pray, trust God, and allow His Spirit to give me wisdom for every conversation with this weak young man.

Choosing to stand in faith, I knew we had a beautiful opportunity to point our son to the cross of Jesus so that he could experience the amazing grace of Jesus. I now see how God used this experience to draw my son to Himself.

I recently sat down with my son, who is now a man, to see if I could share his story and if there were anything he'd like to add. This was his response: "When I watched the pornography as a kid, I thought God couldn't love me anymore. When I was twelve, I couldn't comprehend the danger of sin or the power of forgiveness. Now I know Jesus for myself and trust in His love and grace."

As a momma, there was nothing I could do to teach my son to know Jesus personally. No matter how much I loved him and hoped to shield him from sin, I could not have made the gospel real to him. Our son needed to experience grace for himself. Now I know I was never betrayed by God; I only needed to stand and see how He would bring the victory.

Julie chose to believe that the same loving God, the One who faithfully redeemed her own life from sin and destruction, was more than able to deliver her son. When facing her greatest fear, she had to walk by faith and trust Him even when she could not see how He would turn the darkness to something beautiful. This is what it means to stand.

FAITH BEFORE SIGHT

Often when we hear the word *stand*, we think of our posture or position. Although that is a good definition, the word *stand* is an internal decision of the will rather than only an external physical behavior. It is a call to faith. Only with a heart of faith could Moses look at the obstacles before him and confidently say, "You will see the deliverance the LORD will bring you" (Exod. 14:13).

Just think about the boldness of the phrase "You *will* see." He didn't say "You might see" or "I hope we will see." Nope. By using the future tense, he indicated that this action was certain to occur.

Moses's confidence stood in razor-sharp contrast to the chaos around him. In the natural realm, it appeared that he would be defeated by his circumstances, but actually he was positioned perfectly for the Lord to glorify His name by utterly defeating Pharaoh.

That story comes later.

We must also keep this other crucial fact in mind: in the time preceding God's great display of power over Pharaoh, neither Moses nor the Israelites knew *how* God would deliver them. They didn't have the blessing of Scripture laid out before them, revealing the wondrous deliverance that occurred. No, for them this was a real trial where what they believed about God was put to the test. And what we see in that historic showdown is this:

50

- Faith always comes before sight.
- Faith precedes the miracle.
- Faith always comes before the deliverance.

At the Red Sea, Moses took a stand that has gone down in the history books as the quintessential embodiment of faith in God.

- He did not run.
- He did not bow down.
- He did not hide under the covers and pretend everything was fine.
- He did not compromise the call of God.
- He did not stage a cringe-worthy protest on Facebook.
- He did not beg Pharaoh for mercy.

Instead,

- He stood.
- He believed God.
- He watched with eyes of faith to see what God would do next.

What did Moses have that enabled him to do this? How did he muster this supernatural response in the midst of such dire circumstances? Here's the secret we must learn from Moses: long before his will resolved to stand, his heart determined to believe God.

Believe God.

These two words are absolutely essential to our call to stand. It's not enough that we believe *facts* about Him; we must believe *Him*!

There are moments in life when we must tap into that deep well of faith and allow our beliefs to inform our behavior. Before standing is a posture of the body, it is a determination of the will. Everything in Moses's circumstances screamed doom and devastation, but everything in his heart whispered, "He's got this," and that belief enabled him to stand.

- What seemingly impossible scenario do you face today?
- What mayhem surrounds you?
- What is your Red Sea?

As Christ followers on this journey of faith, we will face various seasons in which we must choose to stand. And I use the word *choose* intentionally. As human beings made in the image of God, we are gifted with a will. The will is our place of decision. This choice is what Scripture speaks of when it says, "Love the LORD your God with all your heart and with all your soul and with all your strength" (Deut. 6:5). Jesus declared this to be the greatest commandment. When we are told to love the Lord with all our heart, soul, and strength, this is our will. This gut-level conviction that God is good, faithful, powerful, and victorious is where the determination to stand is found.

Chapter 2

· · · · · · ·

STAND IN AWE

*Let the whole world fear the LORD, and let
everyone stand in awe of him.*

Psalm 33:8 (NLT)

As we discovered in the story of Shadrach, Meshach, and Abednego
from the introduction, there is an unwavering resolve in the hearts
of people who worship, trust, and love God that enables them to
stand in the midst of the challenges of this world. Our ability to
resist the Enemy, hold our ground, and experience victory is fun-
damentally rooted in our understanding of who our God is. This
resolve to stand is a choice to believe God as we plant our feet on
His character. Before we can stand firm, we must stand in awe of
the Lord. His power, glory, goodness, and majesty must eclipse any
foe or fear we face.

Red Sea moments test our faith. What we truly believe about
God surfaces when life does not go as we planned or when we are

faced with some seemingly impossible obstacles. Is the Lord able, powerful, good, and trustworthy? This is the question that surfaces in our hearts when we are in over our heads. What we discover from Moses's Red Sea experience is that it was his relationship with God, prior to this test, that enabled him to trust Him.

I know this to be true from my own experience. Long before the Red Sea moment I described in the previous chapter, I had already walked through a faith-testing season that rocked my world but ultimately taught me to stand in awe of the Lord's goodness, sovereignty, and love. During that previous test, I was a woman who loved Jesus, studied His Word, and worked in full-time ministry, yet, at the same time, I endured a trial that nearly crushed me. There were many days that I did not stand. Blindsided by a broken heart, disappointed by unmet desires, and struggling to hope, in some moments I could be found in the fetal position on the bathroom floor, questioning God and hosting one heck of a pity party instead of standing firm.

Before that testing season, I would characterize myself as a woman who walked by sight. I wanted to know how God would deliver before I trusted that He would. My faith was weak. My emotions were dictated by my circumstances. As a result, I caved in, over and over again, to despair and hopelessness. One of the primary problems was that my theology prior to that season hadn't prepared me for suffering or spiritual warfare. I was not equipped for those trials because I didn't possess a faith in God that could withstand tests.

When I surrendered my life to Christ in my midtwenties, I often heard people say, "God has a wonderful plan for your life." A decade later, when facing what I perceived to be the painful death of my dreams, that "wonderful plan" seemed nonexistent. I was disillusioned. Questions and accusations thundered against my heart: Does God love me? Does He really have favorable plans for me? If God is really good, why do I hurt so badly?

All the while, I faced an Enemy who relished the thought that I'd bail out on Jesus when life didn't go according to my plan. Satan taunted me with thoughts like this: *So, Marian, how much do you love Jesus now?* Just as the Israelites cried out for Moses to return them to slavery rather than make them face down Pharaoh at the Red Sea, I was tempted to walk away from Jesus when I couldn't comprehend why God allowed certain circumstances in my life.

Single-handedly, the one thing that delivered me from that nearly two-year testing season was a revelation of God's character that birthed a deeper relationship with Him. Before my heartbreak during that time, I knew the Lord based on information I had read about Him in books or heard about Him in sermons, but afterward I knew Him personally. This new knowledge of God was based on real, personal experience.

Jesus carried me every step of that journey. His nearness, power, comfort, and love were no longer theories but rather my ever-present reality as I walked with Him. The psalmist said, "The nearness of God is my good" (Ps. 73:28 NASB). These words are flat-out truth! It was the nearness of God, in my most broken state, that enabled me to see His heart, goodness, and character. He enveloped me and held me in my weakest state. And the Word of God became my lifeline. I held on to biblical truths as though my life depended on them, and in many ways it did. When I couldn't see God moving, the Bible fueled my faith, reminding me of His promises and character, enabling me to stand.

After walking through that previous season of testing and pain, I emerged a different woman: I was more in love with Jesus and more confident in His goodness. No, I didn't see the answers to all my prayers realized, but I did possess a confident hope in God even when I couldn't comprehend His ways. This foundation of faith sustained me and prepared me for future Red Sea moments (much like the night Justin walked out the door, ending our relationship). As my knowledge of God deepened over the years, so did my ability to trust Him.

Moses's understanding of the Lord was the foundation of his faith. This belief was more than just intellectual knowledge. His awe of God was deep in his soul, where faith resides. No threat of Pharaoh, or of any other formidable foe, could rightly compare with the Lord God Almighty, who spoke the world into existence and sustains it by His power.

A HEART ABLAZE

I wonder if in the midst of mayhem at the Red Sea Moses thought back to his first encounter with the Lord. Did he remember the moment when he met the great I AM at the burning bush in the wilderness? That dramatic revelation of the Lord left him awestruck and changed the trajectory of his life. I just wonder if Moses's heart burned hot with a fiery awe, like with the burning-bush experience, when he beheld Pharaoh's army fast on his heels?

Moses was tending the flock of Jethro his father-in-law, the priest of Midian, and he led the flock to the far side of the wilderness and came to Horeb, the mountain of God. There the angel of the LORD appeared to him in flames of fire from within a bush. Moses saw that though the bush was on fire it did not burn up. So Moses thought, "I will go over and see this strange sight—why the bush does not burn up."

When the LORD saw that he had gone over to look, God called to him from within the bush, "Moses! Moses!"

And Moses said, "Here I am."

"Do not come any closer," God said. "Take off your sandals, for the place where you are standing is holy ground." Then he said, "I am the God of your father, the God of Abraham, the God of Isaac and the God of Jacob." At this, Moses hid his face, because he was afraid to look at God.

The LORD said, "I have indeed seen the misery of my people in Egypt. I have heard them crying out because of their slave drivers, and I am concerned about their suffering. So I have come down to rescue them from the hand of the Egyptians and to bring them up out of that land into a good and spacious land, a land flowing with milk and honey—the home of the Canaanites, Hittites, Amorites, Perizzites, Hivites and Jebusites. And now the cry of the Israelites has reached me, and I have seen the way the Egyptians are oppressing them. So now, go. I am sending you to Pharaoh to bring my people the Israelites out of Egypt."

But Moses said to God, "Who am I that I should go to Pharaoh and bring the Israelites out of Egypt?"

And God said, "*I will be with you.* And this will be the sign to you that it is I who have sent you: When you have brought the people out of Egypt, you will worship God on this mountain."

Moses said to God, "Suppose I go to the Israelites and say to them, 'The God of your fathers has sent me to you,' and they ask me, 'What is his name?' Then what shall I tell them?"

God said to Moses, "I AM WHO I AM. This is what you are to say to the Israelites: 'I AM has sent me to you.'"

God also said to Moses, "Say to the Israelites, 'The LORD, the God of your fathers—the God of Abraham, the God of Isaac and the God of Jacob—has sent me to you.'

"This is my name forever,
 the name you shall call me
 from generation to generation."
 (Exod. 3:1–15)

Hands down, that is one of my all-time favorite stories in the Bible. I'm drawn to it, just as Moses was magnetically attracted to the burning bush, because of the revelation we receive here of God's glory and holiness. There is no other God; He alone is the almighty creator and sustainer of life. In our day and age, we've lost a holy reverence and awe of our majestic God, in whose presence we must bow down, take off our sandals, and hide our faces. What we see at the burning bush is a revelation of the Lord that brought about a transformation in Moses.

Stop for a minute and imagine Moses with his hands lifted up to the Holy One at the burning bush. The brilliance of God's majesty seared his inner being, and he was undone. In this encounter, the Lord allowed Moses a glimpse of His glory.

There is a holy awe of God in the Exodus passage that stops me in my tracks, reminding me of the immense mystery and majesty of our great God. Once you've beheld the One and Only, what else matters? Once you've experienced a revelation of the Lord, who holds your next breath and takes it away all at the same time, what is a man that you should fear him? I have to believe that after this encounter, there was no contest in the heart of Moses. The Lord God Almighty had no rival for Moses's heart. Who was Pharaoh in comparison? Let me express this simply: before we can stand before man, our hearts must first burn before God.

I believe that the revelation of God's power and glory at the burning bush prepared Moses to face the Red Sea.

So much about the Lord is learned from this encounter. First of all, God disclosed His name as the great I AM. This name explains His being. He is the self-existent one, who owes His existence to none other. Just let the term *self-existent* roll around in your mind for a minute. Our God, the Creator of all things, owes His existence to no one. He is uncreated and without beginning or end. Therefore, He is without limits or measure. He is all we need!

The name I AM is translated in Scripture as *Jehovah* in Hebrew and *Lord* in English. It is the covenant name of God. It is often linked with other titles to give us a fuller understanding of who He is. Each title is a revelation of His character and commitment to His people:

- Jehovah Sabaoth—I AM your defender.
  (see 1 Sam. 17:45)
- Jehovah Nissi—I AM your victory.
  (see Exod. 17:15)
- Jehovah Ezer—I AM your helper. (see Ps. 33:20)
- Jehovah Jireh—I AM your provider.
  (see Gen. 22:14)
- Jehovah Rapha—I AM your healer.
  (see Exod. 15:26)
- Jehovah Shalom—I AM your peace.
  (see Judg. 6:24)
- Jehovah Nacham—I AM your comforter.
  (see Isa. 51:11–12)

Note how personal and relevant these titles are. The Lord is not some far-removed deity. He is the living God, who is with us as our shield and defender! As we comb through pages of Scripture, we discover these names in the context of His people's needs.

- When we face a mighty army, He is the Lord our victory.
- When we face disease, He is the Lord our healer.
- When we are in the grip of fear, He is the Lord our peace.

God's name, I AM, fits perfectly into whatever circumstance we face. I love how British evangelist and author Roy Hession explained the significance of this name and how knowing Him equips us to stand in the face of specific tests and trials:

> The special revelation which this name gives is that of the Grace of God. "I am" is an unfinished sentence. It has no object. I am—what? What is our wonder when we discover, as we continue with our Bibles, that He is saying, "I AM whatever My people need" and that the sentence is only left blank that man may bring his many and various needs, as they arise, to complete it!...
>
> The name, Jehovah, is really like a blank check. Your faith can fill in what He is to be to you.[1]

At the burning bush, God spoke to Moses's fears and reservations with one assurance:

- I AM here.
- I AM with you.
- I AM trustworthy.

- I AM all-powerful.
- I AM the one who see the tears you cry.
- I AM healer.
- I AM the one who provides a comfort that no amount of alcohol or food can even touch.
- I AM strength.
- I AM enough.

Comprehending the power of God's name helps us see how Moses stood firm at the Red Sea. At the burning-bush encounter, the Lord gave Moses a sure promise of victory. He is our victory, just as Jesus promised us that if we stand firm we will win life. The Lord called Moses to do something that was far beyond his natural ability. Sure, delivering the Hebrew people from slavery in Egypt was more than Moses could handle, but the Lord promised His presence would be with him. It was on this promise of victory that Moses chose to stand.

I STILL BELIEVE

My dear friends Joe and Janelle endured every parent's worst nightmare. Their journey of faith in the midst of suffering is one that has taught me how knowing the Lord personally is the firm foundation upon which we stand when tragedy strikes. Here Janelle describes what happened.

> Just a little over three years ago, I joined my son, Garrett, for Mothers' Weekend with his fraternity. We had a wonderful day full of events for the two

of us, ending with a lovely sit-down dinner. At almost twenty years old and a college sophomore, he was handsome. He was dressed so dapper in his suit and bow tie, but there was also a sense about him. He was nearly a grown man, and I had seen him mature so much since he had left high school. When I dropped him off at his dorm around ten thirty, he leaned in to give me a hug good-bye. Side hugs are even a little more awkward in the front seat of a small car, but as a mom, you never care. Then right as our hug was ending, my sweet boy leaned back in and gave me the sweetest kiss on my cheek. We didn't say anything else except good-bye and "I love you," but my cheek felt warm the whole ride home because it was such a sweet and treasured moment, almost sacred.

The next morning, I came downstairs with the dogs about six thirty to start the coffee, but almost as soon as I entered the kitchen, I thought I heard a tapping at the front door. I went to the front hall, looked out the side window, and saw a policeman standing on our front stoop. Through the door, I asked him if I could help him, as I knew he must be at the wrong door. He said that if my husband were home to please get him. I ran up the stairs and woke my husband while screaming and crying, telling him that a policeman was at the door and needed to speak to us. We both knew what had happened before we ever opened the door to that young policeman early on the morning of November 4.

The horror and disbelief that our beautiful son had died in an incomprehensible accident overwhelmed us immediately. What followed was a blur of phone calls and the arrival of our brave and dear friends and family. By instinct, I held tightly to the anchor of my soul and the promise that my sweet boy was already in heaven in the presence of our God and Savior. But I also knew that with his death, I was no longer a mother and my husband no longer a father. We would never be grandparents; we would never know our daughter-in-law; I would never meet the grandbabies I'd always dreamed I would hold and rock.

Standing is when you look up from the pit of deepest imaginable pain and say, "Yes, I still believe God." Despite the anguish of my soul, I chose to believe. I hated my reality completely and screamed my protests to God that this suffering was too much, but I knew the Lord and trusted Him even when I didn't understand why. This is childlike faith. Standing does not mean soldiering on. That is denial. Standing is real and transparent, revealing to ourselves and others our desperate need for God.

Ever since Garrett died, the Evil One tempts us to just curl up in the dark and wallow in the pain, despair, and loss of hope. But if we are truly children of God, the Word is clear that we can't fall into that trap. We are to stand on the promises of God. If you don't know the Lord before you face your Red Sea moment, you cannot stand upon the promises when darkness descends. If you don't know that He is strong when you are weak, you can't claim that promise as though your next breath depends on it.

The Lord has never been silent or distant and has never left my side. From the minute the policeman knocked on the door that Sunday morning, I have felt His presence so engulfing and His voice whispering, "I am here." The power of His presence does not override the pain; it just allows us to keep standing in the midst of it.

Being children of God does not make us immune to the sufferings of this world; rather, my position as His child enables me to breathe, keep living each day, and stand and see His deliverance.

Faith is not a feeling; it is a confident expectation and hope. For Moses, his unwavering confidence was built upon the power and presence of the Lord. He knew he was not alone in the showdown at the Red Sea; he knew that the Lord God Almighty was with him.

The trajectory of Moses's life changed forever at the burning bush. The encounter established an unwavering reverence and dependence in him. Worship eclipsed worry. The Lord had no rival for his affection or allegiance. Moses's heart was ablaze with a fiery passion forever mimicking the burning bush, and his life was consumed with the will of the One who sent him.

This confident assurance proves the primary difference between Moses and the Hebrew people that fateful day at the Red Sea. Moses's faith was grounded in holy awe, while the Israelites merely knew God from a distance. Moses alone had seen the burning bush, heard the Lord's voice, and learned His name.

Moses knew the heart, character, and purposes of the Lord. The Israelites merely knew stories about Him. There is a vast difference between knowing information about God and actually knowing Him. To know the Lord's ways is to have trust based on experience. Just as I've grown to trust my husband more and more the longer we have been married, so Moses was able to trust the great I AM based on his relationship with Him.

CONFIDENT ASSURANCE

Faith is the choice to trust even when we don't know how God will move. Sometimes faith means we must believe God even when human logic says otherwise and the world thinks we're crazy. So often my Red Sea moments come when I'm forced to trust God even though I can't envision a possible way out of my present situation. Times when my eyes can't see how He will provide or when He will answer my prayer test my faith.

The command Moses gave the people at the Red Sea—stand and see—was not a popular one. If the majority were to have voted, then Moses would have been tossed into the sea. The Hebrew people were desperately afraid, and desperate people don't make smart decisions. Looking back to see Pharaoh's army fast on their heels sent them to the crazy place.

> As Pharaoh approached, the Israelites looked up, and there were the Egyptians, marching after them. They were terrified and cried out to the LORD. They said to Moses, "Was it because there were no graves in Egypt that you brought us to the desert to die? What have you done to us by bringing us out of Egypt? Didn't we say to you in Egypt, 'Leave us alone; let us serve the Egyptians'? It would have been better for us to serve the Egyptians than to die in the desert!" (Exod. 14:10–12)

Note the order of events in this story: First, the Israelites "looked up." Next, they beheld the Egyptians. And then we see the result: "They were terrified." Scripture tells us that the Hebrew people saw the Egyptians and were afraid. As the adage says, "Seeing is believing." This line of reasoning is basic human behavior. All they could see was trouble, and their human logic said, "It is better to be a slave than to die." So they begged Moses to let them return to Egypt, back to the yoke of slavery. Folks, this is Fear 101.

Moses beheld the Lord and believed He would deliver; fixing his eyes on the great I AM, Moses took his stand. Sadly, the opposite was true for the Israelites. Fear had such a grip on their hearts that they were willing to trade the promise of freedom for known slavery. Why? They were more confident in Pharaoh's ability to destroy them than they were in God's ability to deliver them. This is why an awe of God proves so vital to standing firm. Faith conquers fear.

In the book of Hebrews, we find the greatest definition of faith: "Faith is *confidence* in what we hope for and *assurance* about what we do not see.... And without faith it is impossible to please God, because anyone who comes to him must believe that he exists and that he rewards those who earnestly seek him" (Heb. 11:1, 6). Those two words, *confidence* and *assurance*, are a powerful combo. If there is one thing the human heart craves, it is confident assurance. So much of our time, money, energy, and investments go into trying to attain this sense of security. We work to secure a life we think will withstand financial hardship. We spend our energy trying to control relationships so that we feel confident that we are loved. We spend our money purchasing products we hope will shelter us from life's storms. All of this striving and control is rooted in fear. Often we don't have faith that we are beloved children of God and as such will never be abandoned or forsaken; therefore, we fight, strive, perform, and manipulate in order to gain assurance that we are safe. These efforts often prove futile, as there is never enough money or possessions, nor is there a human relationship that can ultimately quiet our fears and speak confidence to our hearts.

What God is continually trying to reveal is that the only safe place, the only unshakable foundation, is Him. All other safety nets will fail, but God never will. All too often we look to people, careers, and other comforts to be our confident assurance, but those things are never able to deliver us from the Pharaohs we face. Only when we place our full hope in Jesus do we know the type of supernatural peace that comes from authentic faith.

This kind of faith is found only in a real relationship with God. Just as Moses knew God personally and trusted Him, we must also know Him in order to remain steadfast when calamity strikes.

During the early years of my relationship with God, I did not possess the type of faith that stands firm. My emotional well-being was built upon the flimsy foundation of my circumstances. I rode up and down the emotional roller coaster based on the factors of the day. If you'd asked me, I would have heartily told you I had faith. Sure, I believed facts about God, but deep in my belly, where fear and faith duked it out for dominance, I caved in to fear on too many occasions. My confidence rested wholly in what my eyes could see. And if my eyes didn't see a particular promise fulfilled, need provided, or victory assured, then I didn't stand.

The word *stand* is a very personal one. As I've shared, my journey with Jesus began in my midtwenties. Before that, I was a complete train wreck. Redeemed from a life of sin and rebellion, I came to faith with a backstory of brokenness and emptiness. A fragile, hurting girl with a tough exterior, I was one small push from falling almost every day. Along the way, I discovered that faith is muscle. It grows. It gets stronger. Like strength training of the physical body, life's circumstances train our spiritual muscles to stand.

As I've walked with Jesus, He's proven His heart, goodness, faithfulness, and power time and time again. In my nearly two decades of following Christ, He has not only healed the girl I once was but has also taught me to be a woman who stands.

Day by day, faith-mustering moment by faith-mustering moment, I've learned to trust God. I'm not saying I do it perfectly—absolutely not! But what I am confessing is that over the years, my faith muscles have grown. Situations that sent me spiraling a few years ago are the building blocks of faith for my heart today:

- The times when God provided for me financially taught me to trust Him with my future needs.
- The time when God protected me from a bad relationship taught me to surrender my plans and desires to His will.
- The seasons in which I grew to comprehend God's sovereignty equipped me for when life didn't go as I planned.
- The times when God delivered me from sin's destruction taught me to listen and obey His voice when temptation strikes.

There is a cumulative effect that happens as we find ourselves in situations where we are forced to stand. What we learn about God during one season equips us for the next.

Faith is not an intellectual assent that agrees with a particular set of doctrine; it is an internal resolve that hopes in God. When our hearts stand in awe of Him, we in turn trust Him. The Israelites believed many things about God. They too witnessed His miracles and heard the stories, but when faced with their Red Sea moment, their fear proved that they held a greater awe of Pharaoh than they did of the Lord. Their bitter response and angry outburst was evidence of the condition of their hearts: although they believed in God, they didn't trust Him. Moses, however, exhibited trust based on a proven relationship.

What about you? What do your emotions reveal about your faith? All too often, when I have an ugly outburst of anger or feel weighed down by worry, I have to stop and examine my faith and ask myself tough questions: Am I trusting God right now? Do I believe He is good? Do I think this situation is bigger than God's ability to handle it?

Learning about Moses teaches us the power of awe. Instead of focusing on the approaching enemy, he set his eyes on God, believing in what He could do even when faced with the impossible. With eyes of faith, Moses chose to stand and see.

> Moses answered the people, "Do not be afraid. Stand firm and you will see the deliverance the LORD will bring you today. The Egyptians you see today you will never see again. The LORD will fight for you; you need only to be still." (Exod. 14:13–14)

Moses told Israel, "Do not be afraid.... The LORD will fight for you." What a beautiful promise. What a glorious truth for a child of God to hold dear. When facing our greatest fears, when surrounded by impossible situations, when the deck is stacked against us, we can rein in our emotions with the assurance that the Lord fights for us.

Friends, I get it. Sometimes we don't have enough strength or courage to even get out of bed. What do we do when we can't stand? Here's the beautiful thing about our God: He equips us with what we do not have when we simply ask. He gives us faith to believe. We can ask the Lord to deepen our awe of Him so that we can stand and see when our fears scream, "Run and hide!"

There have been countless times that I've faced Red Sea moments and didn't have the faith to stand firm. In those times, I've cried out for God to help me believe and hold fast to Him. I've begged Him to strengthen my faith and give me a deeper revelation of His power, love, and faithfulness that calms my fears and quiets the crazy. He is faithful! Often the greatest battle lies within us, not outside us. When we cry out to Him for help and experience the supernatural covering of His presence, we are enabled to stand in moments that testify that God is with us.

Chapter 3

. . . .

HE'S GOT THIS

Faith is deliberate confidence in the character of God
whose ways you may not understand at the time.

Oswald Chambers

The night Justin ended our relationship and the Lord called me to stand, I did not know what the outcome would be or how God would deliver. Sure, I knew the Scripture reference and Moses's Red Sea experience, but knowing about a Bible story is a far cry from actually having to walk it out. That night, the Lord wanted me to believe Him and trust that He was with me, working all of this for my good and His glory. As I shared in the previous chapter, I had already walked through a devastating season of heartbreak before, and as I faced the possibility of yet another bitter disappointment, I felt my knees buckle. The temptation to succumb to fear and depression knocked at my door, but more loudly than the siren call of self-pity was the strong voice of my God, who said, "Stand … and see" (2 Chron. 20:17).

I know that the only reason I was able to heed this call was that I cried out to Jesus for His help and power to do so. When I did, I experienced the covering of His presence. The Lord was with me, strengthening my feeble knees, enabling me to stand.

I was surprised at the peace that shielded me. To say that my faith muscles had grown over the years is an understatement. Looking back at the woman I was before, I knew that the old Marian easily would have had a full-blown meltdown on the floor, crying her eyes out and cowering to fear of the unknown future, escaping into a Netflix-and-ice-cream coma for weeks on end. I fully expected an emotional outburst rivaling the Israelites' panic attack at the Red Sea, yet something seismic had shifted in my soul. The girl who once crumbled at the thought of her plans not being realized was replaced with a woman who trusted God, even when the outcome was unknown.

I felt the Lord's presence so keenly the night Justin left. I sensed He was shielding me, just as He had the Israelites from Pharaoh's army. His love enveloped me, and I found myself surprised at my ability to not cave in to the fears and doubts. I kept thinking, *Perhaps I'm in shock and I'll go into meltdown mode in a minute.* But that didn't happen. Something deep within my soul believed that the Lord would work this for good. I just didn't know how.

As I sat on my bed, preparing for what I assumed would be an all-night crying session, I opened my Bible. I flipped to a place bookmarked with a single scrap of paper that read, "He's got this!" A knowing smile formed on my face. Wow, what timing!

I knew the handwriting immediately. A friend must have slipped the note in my Bible at some earlier date. But that night, staring down at the page, I knew it was a word directly to my heart from God. The Lord wanted me to stand and believe—but not in any particular outcome. He wanted me to trust that, in all things, He's got this. With that reminder, a fresh surge of peace flooded my heart. I didn't need to worry or panic—Jesus had my back.

I knew two truths that enabled my heart to stand: First, I was never promised a future with Justin that would lead to marriage, so there was a good chance that I was facing life without him. Second, I knew I would still be okay, even if I were alone. I peered into the future and imagined my life without Justin. I acknowledged that the heartbreak would be painful for a season but that I would eventually heal. It wasn't because I didn't love him or want to marry him; it was because I knew that Jesus would be with me whether I was married or single. I would never walk alone. The Lord had been so faithful in the past; I knew that even if my future did not include marriage, it did include Jesus. Because of that, I would be okay.

Satan, our Enemy, always operates in the realm of fear. He loves to project future scenarios minus the presence of God. When he does this, we tend to panic and lose hope. We can't see how we will manage or make it through the Red Sea. But faith chooses to see God in every equation. Sure, I faced the possibility of a broken heart and crushed dreams, but the one thing that my Enemy didn't include in his projections of the future was how Jesus would be with me, carrying me through each day and providing everything my heart needed in order to overcome.

As my trust in the Lord had grown over the years, I was able to face the potential fears with the belief that my life was in the hands of my good, faithful, and trustworthy heavenly Father. He was fighting for me. He would never leave me nor forsake me. Just as Moses's confidence in the Lord was based upon experience, so my trust in Jesus had grown over the years, equipping me to believe Him in my darkest hour. I knew if Justin was the Lord's very best match for me, God Himself would fight our battle and bring victory. I trusted that Justin listened to God and that this battle was not over until the Lord said it was over. I slept well that night, comforted by the presence of God and snuggled tight in His peace. I closed my eyes with one phrase ringing in my ears: "He's got this."

THE MIRACLE

Here's what we need to learn from Moses's Red Sea moment. God strategically positioned His people so that He could show off a crushing defeat of their enemy. The Lord allowed Pharaoh to pursue the Israelites to the Red Sea so that He could display His mighty power to deliver in such a way that none present would ever forget. His sovereignty worked to bring about their deliverance and left no doubt of who would get the glory.

But, oh, those anxious minutes that ticked by as the children of Israel waited for the miracle. That space of time between our needs and God's deliverance is where we are forced to stand. For the Hebrew people, the hoofbeats of Pharaoh's army grew louder and the Red Sea loomed larger before they witnessed the unveiling of God's miraculous plan.

- In God's economy, it is faith first, miracles second.
- Faith believes when it does not see the provision.
- Faith waits and watches for the miracle.

Sometimes that space of time is mere minutes, and for other situations it may be a lifetime of waiting, but the call to stand and see God's deliverance is the same for all of us. We never know how He will work our most painful testing seasons for our good and His glory. Our call is to trust Him and believe that He will.

Now we come to the point in the Exodus story when Moses's faith became sight. Although his decision to stand firm at the Red Sea seemed counterintuitive, it was not counterproductive. He did not know how the Lord would deliver; he just believed that He would.

> The angel of God, who had been traveling in front of Israel's army, withdrew and went behind them. The pillar of cloud also moved from in front and stood behind them, coming between the armies of Egypt and Israel. Throughout the night the cloud brought darkness to the one side and light to the other side; so neither went near the other all night long. (Exod. 14:19–20)

Imagine being there with the Israelites as they watched the glorious cloud, which was the presence of God, strategically move to stand between them and their enemy. He literally had their backs! God's very presence was with His people. What a crucial message for us as we encounter faith-testing seasons. He is with us! The Lord

God Almighty has our backs. Just as He hovered above the Israelites in a cloud by day and fire by night, He is with you right now in whatever you're facing.

- You are not battling this illness alone.
- You are not enduring this heartbreak alone.
- You are not walking through this family crisis alone.
- You are not facing unemployment alone.
- You are not facing _____ alone.
- Take heart. You are not at your Red Sea alone.

Jesus is Emmanuel; this name means "God with us" (Matt. 1:23). He is with you. God's presence provides what no pill or substance can give us. The Lord gives us peace, joy, confidence, and power when we are bankrupt of any of these in our own strength. It was confidence born from God's presence that enabled Moses to act boldly in the face of such significant obstacles.

> Moses stretched out his hand over the sea, and all that night the LORD drove the sea back with a strong east wind and turned it into dry land. *The waters were divided, and the Israelites went through the sea on dry ground, with a wall of water on their right and on their left.* (Exod. 14:21–22)

Dry ground. Just let those two words roll around in your mind for a minute. Just try to comprehend the weight of that reality: a sea became a highway. The Hebrew people marched forward, with a wall of water on their right and on their left and with the cloud of God's presence guarding them from the rear. As if that was not enough, He caused the ground where the water had been to become completely dry. We can easily skim over those words and lose sight of the truly miraculous event that occurred. Not only did God make a way, but He also smoothed the way.

Try to envision that instant when Moses's faith became sight. He knew that God would deliver them; he just didn't know He would show off in such a powerful way. I imagine the moment the people took their first steps off the shore and through the Red Sea. Did they tiptoe or sprint for the Promised Land? Awestruck by the wall of water on their right and left, I imagine there was quite the pileup at the opening as they stood in awe of God's glorious display of power.

What an incredible moment it must have been when forward to freedom the Israelites marched on dry ground. Their enemy, however, still had not learned his lesson. Pharaoh and his army had to learn the hard way that God fights for His people!

> The Egyptians pursued them, and all Pharaoh's horses and chariots and horsemen followed them into the sea. During the last watch of the night the LORD looked down from the pillar of fire and cloud at the Egyptian army and threw it into confusion. He jammed the wheels of their chariots so that they had difficulty driving. And the Egyptians said, "Let's get away from the Israelites! The LORD is fighting for them against Egypt." (Exod. 14:23–25)

Friends, there are moments in life where God works on our behalf in ways we can never begin to imagine. If you are His child, He is for you, not against you. He loves you and will work all things for your good and His glory. Even when the Enemy pursues, the Lord will ultimately be victorious.

> The LORD said to Moses, "Stretch out your hand over the sea so that the waters may flow back over the Egyptians and their chariots and horsemen." Moses stretched out his hand over the sea, and at daybreak the sea went back to its place. The Egyptians were fleeing toward it, and the LORD swept them into the sea. The water flowed back and covered the chariots and horsemen—the entire army of Pharaoh that had followed the Israelites into the sea. Not one of them survived.
>
> *But the Israelites went through the sea on dry ground,* with a wall of water on their right and on their left. That day the LORD saved Israel from the hands of the Egyptians, and Israel saw the Egyptians lying dead on the shore. And when the Israelites saw the mighty hand of the LORD displayed against the Egyptians, the people feared the LORD and put their trust in him and in Moses his servant. (Exod. 14:26–31)

Great is His faithfulness!
God promised!
God delivered!

To the Israelites, the Lord was their guiding light, but to their enemies, He was a blanket of darkness. Not only did He protect them, but with a mighty display of His power He also drove back the waters of the Red Sea.

There was not a single thing Moses did to conjure up this spectacular deliverance except to stand and see. Each step through the wall of water was purely a step of faith, trusting that God would see them through to the end and sustain the miracle until the very last mother holding her child stepped onto freedom's land.

THE LORD FIGHTS FOR US

The night Justin walked out the door, I slept soundly. Like the cloud of God's presence, a supernatural calm covered me. Meanwhile, across town, Justin experienced a far different evening. He was under serious attack from the Enemy. This was his Red Sea moment. Unable to sleep, he fought his fears and doubts throughout the night. He cried out to God for help, and the Lord answered.

The next morning, Justin called me and asked if he could come back over to talk again. He hinted that the Lord had done something in his heart overnight. Within an hour, he was back at my front door, this time a far different man from the one I had seen the night before. Eyes puffy from a sleepless night, he asked me to take a walk. As we walked side by side, he shared with me his word from the Lord. I bet you can guess it: *stand*.

He told me that he had called three godly men—men he respected as mentors—and asked their advice. Each one had responded to Justin's fears and doubts with one simple word: *stand*.

They told him that faith means we choose to believe God even when our fears scream otherwise. While Justin wasn't one of those guys who was afraid of commitment, he was facing a real battle with a real Enemy who wanted to keep him from God's best. They reminded him of how Moses called Israel to stand and see the deliverance of the Lord.

In the wee hours of the morning, while I slept, God moved. The Lord didn't need my help. He gave Justin the same word that He'd given me just hours before. For Justin, the word *stand* meant he was not to let the Enemy win. Instead, he was to trust God with each step forward into the unknown. The Enemy, who hates marriage, didn't want us to take that next step, so he was attacking Justin with every fiery dart in his arsenal. Lies of failure and fear rained down all night, but in the midst of the firestorm, the Lord said, "Stand and see."

Of course, I couldn't believe it when I learned that the Lord had given us the same word! But reflecting back on that night, my biggest takeaway was how the great I AM worked while I slept. I very well could have thrown a major tantrum or freaked out in fear, but I'm thankful the Lord called me to trust Him as He dealt with Justin. He fights for us! He is the God of angel armies. He never leaves us nor forsakes us. When we entrust our lives to Him, He is faithful.

A few short months later, Justin and I stood hand in hand, this time at an altar. Pledging covenant love to each another, we experienced the victory of that fateful night by becoming husband and wife. Our wedding was the best day of my life. I know every girl hopes for that, but I have never experienced the presence of God as I did that day. My family's old barn nestled on a hilltop in East Texas became holy ground. God was there. It was glorious.

In the minutes after saying our vows together, Justin and I knelt at the altar and prayed. While we prayed, our friends led the congregation in the worship song "The Stand" by Hillsong United. If you aren't familiar with the song, please download it. The words beautifully express the cry of our heart that day: "I'll stand with arms high and heart abandoned in awe of the One who gave it all."[1]

The word *stand* was the anthem of our hearts, and we longed for it to be the music of our marriage. As the worship team sang these words, I looked back from the altar to see a spontaneous outbreak of praise. One by one, our guests began to stand and lift hands high to God, bearing stories of deliverance and proclaiming from grateful hearts how the Lord had fought for them in their weakness. What I discovered when I looked back to see worship breaking out was this: *stand* was not just my word; it is our word. It belongs to the bride of Christ.

Friends, standing firm is the posture of our faith. It is the decision of the will to believe God. Although He doesn't always deliver overnight or even in this lifetime, we must trust Him even when we can't see the outcome or how He will work a situation for our good.

Faith is the spiritual muscle that enables us to stand. As we move forward in our study and learn to hold fast to Jesus in the midst of darkness, temptation, and persecution, may your confidence in God's power, love, and goodness embolden you to hold your ground. Lift up your spiritual eyes and behold the God who is with you and will never forsake you. Take your stand in the fact that He's got this.

STAND

· · · · · · · · · · ·

THE PLANTED FEET

To Him who can keep you on your feet, standing tall in his bright presence, fresh and celebrating—to our one God, our only Savior, through Jesus Christ, our Master, be glory, majesty, strength, and rule before all time, and now, and to the end of all time.

Jude 24–25 (THE MESSAGE)

Chapter 4

ON CHRIST THE SOLID ROCK I STAND

The LORD is my rock, my fortress and my deliverer;
my God is my rock, in whom I take refuge, my shield
and the horn of my salvation, my stronghold.

Psalm 18:2

For nearly fifteen years I lived in Houston. Humidity and concrete aside, I adore that city—the people, the food, the energy. It helps that I first fell in love with Jesus, surrendered my life to Him, and experienced radical transformation in that city. My spiritual foundation was built in that thriving Texas boomtown. Today I am blessed to call San Antonio my home, but Houston will always hold a special place in my heart.

One thing you need to know about Houston is that it is called the Bayou City. This name stems from the fact that it is built around and upon a swamp. Streaming through this great metropolis are several bayous (or small rivers, for those of you who don't speak Cajun), which cause severe flooding when the rains descend (as they are apt to do).

The other big issue Houstonians must deal with is foundation problems. The rise and fall of the water level can cause slabs to shift and move over time. The evidence of shifting soil appears in cracks on walls, doors that don't close properly, and bulging floors. These warning signs raise a big red flag that something is majorly wrong.

Just as our homes can give us warning signs that the foundation is faulty, so can our lives. If we build our lives on an unstable base, then we too will exhibit cracks and not function properly. For us to become men and women who stand firm, we must build our lives on the only foundation that proves secure and unshakable until the end: Jesus Christ.

One of Jesus's most famous parables teaches us about the importance of building our lives upon the rock. This parable is found at the conclusion of the Sermon on the Mount, which theologians believe encapsulates His teachings on the kingdom of God.

> Everyone who hears these words of mine and puts them into practice is like a wise man who built his house on the rock. The rain came down, the streams rose, and the winds blew and beat against that house; yet it did not fall, because it had its foundation on the rock. But everyone who hears these words of mine and does not put them into practice is like a foolish man who built his house

on sand. The rain came down, the streams rose, and the winds blew and beat against that house, and it fell with a great crash. (Matt. 7:24–27)

Jesus was the master teacher. He commonly utilized the ordinary to illustrate the sacred. In this parable, he compared two different builders: the wise and the foolish. Keep in mind that these men have two things in common: both will build houses, and both will face tumultuous obstacles such as winds, rains, storms, and floods. These difficulties represent the trials and heartache we all encounter. No one is immune to life's storms. The question is, how will we stand against them?

Jesus called one builder foolish and the other one wise. So what is the difference between the two? The game changer was the choice of foundation. The foolish one built his house on the sand, which resulted in a great crash. However, the wise builder was praised for building his house on the rock. These builders represent you and me. Each one of us will choose the type of foundation our lives are built upon. The storms of life will come: health crises, financial setbacks, family drama, and personal loss. The question isn't if we will face a storm; it's if we will withstand one. Jesus said the wise person chooses to build on the rock.

Throughout the Bible, a rock is a symbol of God. It signifies His strength, security, and stability as our strong foundation.

Who is God besides the LORD?
And who is the *Rock* except our God?
(2 Sam. 22:32)

In You, O LORD, I have taken refuge;

Let me never be ashamed;

In Your righteousness deliver me.

Incline Your ear to me, rescue me quickly;

Be to me a *rock of strength*,

A stronghold to save me.

For *You are my rock* and my fortress;

For Your name's sake You will lead me and

　　　　　guide me. (Ps. 31:1–3 NASB)

O come, let us sing for joy to the LORD,

Let us shout joyfully to *the rock of our salvation*.

　　　(95:1 NASB)

This parable has a double meaning. First, Jesus is the rock. When we build our lives upon Him, we have a strong foundation. Second, Jesus speaks of His teachings, which form the bedrock for one who stands firm to the end. Over the course of this chapter and the next, we will discover how to plant our feet on Christ, our Solid Rock, and how to stand firm on the sure foundation of His Word. What I've discovered is that before we can withstand the external forces that seek to topple us, our feet must be firmly planted on the person and words of Jesus Christ.

FEET PLANTED ON THE SOLID ROCK

I've been honored to share my redemption story with men and women across the world. It gives me unspeakable joy to tell of the transforming power of the gospel. Today I'm clean, whole, and forgiven, which is why, nearly two decades later, I still call myself a Redeemed Girl.

Whenever I tell my story, I use "The Solid Rock," one of my favorite hymns, as an illustration. The composer, Edward Mote, was a street kid from an irreligious family. At the age of eighteen, he trusted Christ and went on to write more than one hundred hymns. The first stanza describes God's grace, while the second and third illustrate an application of grace in times of trouble.

> My hope is built on nothing less
> Than Jesus's blood and righteousness;
> I dare not trust the sweetest frame,
> But wholly lean on Jesus's name.
> On Christ, the solid rock, I stand;
> All other ground is sinking sand,
> All other ground is sinking sand.[1]

Where do we stand? On Christ, the Solid Rock! Because *all* other ground is sinking sand. Sinking sand could include such things as education, money, popularity, wealth, fame, striving for perfection, and religion devoid of relationship with God. These things, although not evil, are sinking because they are not substantial enough to support our lives.

This hymn perfectly illustrates my life before and after Jesus. Before Jesus, I sought to fill the God-shaped hole in my soul with relationships, substances, and everything the world advertises for happiness and pleasure. Nothing in this world could fill that empty vacuum, and the reason is that I wasn't created to find life in any of those things. We are created by God for relationship with Him. Real life is found only in Jesus. I experienced the destruction of attempting to build my life on sinking sand. My life was built upon the fickle things the world values: beauty, popularity, substances, romantic love, money, and success. Primarily, I was trusting in myself and never knew real peace.

Then I heard the gospel of grace and surrendered my life to Jesus Christ. Coming to Him from rampant sin and utter brokenness left me with little confidence in myself. Let's just say I didn't struggle with self-righteousness. I knew without a shadow of a doubt that I couldn't stand before a holy God. Nothing about my life felt righteous or holy. Psalm 130:3 says, "If you, LORD, kept a record of sins, Lord, who could stand?" I knew I could not stand before a holy God if He kept a record of sin. Thankfully, the gift of grace offered to me by Jesus was good news to this sinner's ears.

If I could sum up the amazing grace of God in one thought, it would be this: we can stand before a holy God only because His Son stands in the gap for us. Understanding the fullness of the gospel is essential for us as we learn to stand firm in all areas of life. If we aren't confident in our position before God, then our ability to remain steadfast in trials, temptations, and persecutions will be weakened. When our feet are planted on the Rock, we are confident to stand against the storms of life. Jesus, only Jesus, is our strong foundation. Christ alone is the rock upon which we stand during the storms of life. This is summed up beautifully in the next two stanzas:

When darkness veils His lovely face,
I rest on His unchanging grace;
In every high and stormy gale,
My anchor holds within the veil.

His oath, His covenant, His blood
Support me in the whelming flood;
When all around my soul gives way,
He then is all my hope and stay.

As Jesus warned us, even the wise builder will face the storms of life. There will be difficult times when "darkness veils His lovely face." Seasons of sickness or sorrow may send our souls into grief, but take heart: Jesus never leaves us nor forsakes us. He is our firm foundation in the storm. In whatever "whelming flood" seeks to destroy us, Jesus is our "hope and stay." Just as Moses stood firm in the face of Pharaoh, trusting in his relationship with the Lord, so do we! There is a vast difference between religion and knowing Jesus. When our feet are planted on the Solid Rock, the storms will strike but we will stand.

As encouraging as those lines are to my soul, it is the last stanza that keeps me sane and holds my heart steady when I see my garbage and know that I'm still a work in progress. Even on our best days, we are desperate for Jesus.

When He shall come with trumpet sound,
O, may I then in Him be found;

Dressed in His righteousness alone,

Faultless to stand before the throne.

Let me ask you: Have you ever felt unworthy to stand before God? Have you ever heard a voice whispering words of shame and reminding you of your sin? Have you ever doubted God's love for you?

I know I have listened to these taunts many times. One area in which our faith is often attacked is the realm of shame. Friends, we have an Enemy, one the Bible calls "the accuser of our brothers and sisters" (Rev. 12:10). He loves to remind us that we are far from "faultless to stand before the throne." This Enemy specializes in hurling accusations at us. Why? Satan knows that when we are loaded with shame and weighed down with the burden of sin, the last thing in the world we want to do is stand in the face of darkness, temptation, and persecution. Planting our feet firmly on the Solid Rock, believing we are righteous before God, enables us to hold our ground when we face these overwhelming floods.

ROBED IN RIGHTEOUSNESS

Not even on our best days, on our best behavior, has our status as children of God been based upon our merit. We are wholly and woefully in need of God's grace. We are dependent upon the outpouring of mercy found in Christ alone, our Cornerstone. We stand because He stands for us!

I love how "The Solid Rock" uses the metaphor of clothing to symbolize our redeemed status as God's beloved children. Close your eyes for a minute and envision yourself dressed in Jesus's righteousness, standing faultless, blameless, holy, and beloved before the throne of God. That's who you are! Imagine the Lord taking away your tattered garments that are stained with lies, lust, pride, jealousy, hypocrisy, anger, addictions, pornography, adultery (or whatever specific brand of sin or shame you carry) and replacing these old rags with the radiant, holy, and glorious perfection of His Son, Jesus. This is what it means to be robed in righteousness. And lest you think I'm reading too much theology into a hymn, let's take a look at Scripture:

> I delight greatly in the LORD;
>   my soul rejoices in my God.
> For he has clothed me with garments of salvation
>   and arrayed me in a robe of his righteousness.
>   (Isa. 61:10)

To be arrayed in a robe of righteousness means to be fully covered by the perfect life of Jesus. The sinless, blameless, God-pleasing life of Christ covers us. Why does this matter? This truth is the game-changing, life-altering, Satan-kicking, freedom-giving, best news of all time. What years of religion and rule keeping could never do, Jesus did.

One of the best illustrations of this truth is the parable of the prodigal son found in Luke 15:11–32. In this story, Jesus tells of a young man who rejected his father and squandered his inheritance in sin and wild living, only to wake up wallowing in the consequences of his rebellion. This kid wasted his life and inheritance on one big frat party in Vegas. What he envisioned would be life and freedom actually resulted in brokenness and destruction. Filled with shame and regret, he devised a plan to go home and make things right with his father.

Smelling like sewage, covered in mud and pig food, the young man made his journey home. (Let me jump ahead to the punch line: this kid represents you and me. We are all covered in sin, shame, and the stench of our pasts.) On his journey home, the young man prepared a speech to tell his father. I'm sure we've all rehearsed speeches like his before: "I'll be better next time." "I'm such a failure." "This time, God, I'll be good."

Let's pick up the story from the text and see how the father responded to the prodigal son.

> He got up and went to his father.
>
> But while he was still a long way off, his father saw him and was filled with compassion for him; he ran to his son, threw his arms around him and kissed him.
>
> The son said to him, "Father, I have sinned against heaven and against you. I am no longer worthy to be called your son."
>
> But the father said to his servants, "Quick! Bring the best robe and put it on him. Put a ring on his finger and sandals on his feet. Bring the fattened calf and kill it. Let's have a feast and celebrate. For this son of mine was dead and is alive again; he was lost and is found." So they began to celebrate. (Luke 15:20–24)

In perfect Jesus fashion, this story did not end as anyone expected. The young man didn't give his well-crafted speech or try to make things right. The father didn't punish him or reject him. Actually, the Bible tells us that while the son was still a long way off, the father saw him and ran to him. He ran to him! Embraced him. Showered him with love.

Friends, you and I are that son.

What a beautiful picture of the grace of God. Jesus uses this story to illustrate the love of our heavenly Father and demonstrate how He wants relationship with us even when we are messes, even when we've squandered everything on wild living. But the story doesn't end there. The father does something extraordinary: he covers his son with new clothes. He removes the filthy stench of his past and covers him with a clean, fresh robe of righteousness: "See what great love the Father has lavished on us, that we should be called children of God!" (1 John 3:1).

The robe represented membership in the family. It spoke acceptance when rejection was what was expected. This garment symbolized the son's restoration to his father's house. Ironically, the prodigal son left home thinking he would discover the party life, but only in returning home and experiencing grace did he get welcomed into the real party. The same is true of us. Our heavenly Father has welcomed us into His family and covered us with the robe of righteousness, Jesus Christ. It is in this amazing place of love and acceptance that we are invited into the greatest feast of all.

I want to speak this word of grace to every person reading this today. It doesn't matter what you've done in your past or what sin you are weighed down by today. You are redeemed! And this is the truth upon which we stand.

It doesn't matter if your dirty rags are adultery, pornography, homosexuality, lying, murder, rage, or jealousy. When Jesus conquered sin and death on the cross, He flung the doors of your prison cell wide open. Because of Christ, we are lavished with garments of amazing grace, and this is what our heavenly Father says:

- You are not excluded; you are beloved.
- You are not rejected; you are accepted.
- You are not forgotten; you are chosen.

Rise up and stand redeemed. Behold, how deep the Father's love for us!

There is only one response to this lavish grace found in Jesus Christ: we abandon all and follow Him! It would be insane for the prodigal son to return home and remain covered in the pig-stained clothing of his past. The same applies to us. When we comprehend that the God of the universe has chosen us to be His own, paid the highest price possible to set us free, and lavishes us with garments of grace, it is crazy to think that we would go on living in the same bondage and brokenness that was ours before. The one who is redeemed by Jesus lives for Jesus. Let's plant our feet firmly in the grace of God found in Jesus Christ and stand firm, forgiven, and free!

What difference does knowing we are forgiven and free make when it comes to standing firm? How does believing we are righteous and beloved by God enable us to hold our ground in seasons of darkness, temptation, and persecution? In the upcoming chapters, we will discover how our identity in Christ and our confidence that we are righteous before God prove critical to utilizing the armor of God, which we take up against the spiritual forces of darkness. Friends, before we can stand our ground in the midst of spiritual warfare or persecution, we must first believe the fundamental truth of who we are in Christ: we are His!

Chapter 5

• • • • • • •

ALL OTHER GROUND
IS SINKING SAND

*The grass withers and the flowers fade, but
the word of our God stands forever.*

Isaiah 40:8 (NLT)

Weary from working all night, with nothing but empty nets to show for their labor, a few beaten-down fishermen dragged their boats to shore as the first light of dawn broke the morning mist. As professional fishermen, they were accustomed to their routine. Fish at night. Rest during the day. Hope for a catch and make a little money if the night's work produced a profit. They'd followed this proven routine all their lives as their fathers and the ones before them had done. Fishing was in their DNA.

Their well-worn plan didn't pan out that night. Dragging nets to shore this dawn, these seasoned fishermen were downcast. Their hard work and sleepless night produced nothing. *Empty.* What a word. Their empty nets mocked them from shore—not even a single fish.

Then Jesus of Nazareth, the rabbi they'd heard about, was there preaching to the masses from the shore of Galilee. You've got to give Jesus credit. In a day and age without technology or microphones, the coastline provided the perfect amphitheater for the masses to sit and hear His words. Overflowing the grassy coastline, the crowds pressed close until He needed more room to preach. Looking to Simon (who would soon be named Peter), Jesus asked a favor. This moment, this awe-filled encounter, would change the trajectory of Peter's life forever.

> One day as Jesus was standing by the Lake of Gennesaret, the people were crowding around him and listening to the word of God. He saw at the water's edge two boats, left there by the fishermen, who were washing their nets. He got into one of the boats, the one belonging to Simon, and asked him to put out a little from shore. Then he sat down and taught the people from the boat.
>
> When he had finished speaking, he said to Simon, "Put out into deep water, and let down the nets for a catch."
>
> Simon answered, "Master, we've worked hard all night and haven't caught anything. But because you say so, I will let down the nets."
>
> When they had done so, they caught such a large number of fish that their nets began to break. So they signaled their partners in the other boat to

come and help them, and they came and filled both boats so full that they began to sink.

When Simon Peter saw this, he fell at Jesus' knees and said, "Go away from me, Lord; I am a sinful man!" For he and all his companions were astonished at the catch of fish they had taken, and so were James and John, the sons of Zebedee, Simon's partners.

Then Jesus said to Simon, "Don't be afraid; from now on you will fish for people." So they pulled their boats up on shore, *left everything and followed him.* (Luke 5:1–11)

Although these fishermen had worked all night and caught nothing, at Jesus's command Peter returned to the water, let down the nets, and waited. Somewhere between the command and the obedience, the supernatural occurred. Their boat began to sink and their nets began to break because the miraculous catch of fish was so massive that it could not be contained.

Absolute awe and fear filled Peter. He knew this was a miracle. He'd just spent a fruitless night on these same waters and caught nothing. He also recognized that this miracle occurred by obedience to the word of one man, Jesus Christ.

Facedown, Peter fell at Jesus's feet. How else does one respond to a blatant display of power and authority over even the fish of the sea?

- You bow to the One who is the speaker of life.
- You bow to the One who reigns over creation.
- You bow to the One who overflows the empty.

Undone by majesty, Peter recognized his sinfulness and, yes, emptiness. Don't let the symbolism slip by undetected. This soldier of the sea experienced life without Jesus in the boat as well as life with Jesus. The first came up hollow, and the later was so full that it overflowed to the point of breaking. This miracle spoke volumes to Peter. There was only One who was worthy of his life, and that was Jesus Christ.

Scripture tells us that Peter and his companions left everything to follow Jesus. They made the pivotal decision to establish their lives on His teachings and stand upon His words. We call these men disciples. The word *disciple* means follower, learner, or apprentice. The role of a disciple is to learn from and imitate the master. These fishermen and others like them abandoned family, friends, careers, parental expectations, and security to follow the One whose words ripped through their souls and brought life eternal.

When Jesus taught, it was His disciples who sat at His feet, absorbing every word. There would be no disconnect between hearing the words of Jesus and doing the words of Jesus. Therefore, when Jesus taught the parable of the wise builder, which we began studying in the previous chapter, He did so to those who had abandoned everything to follow Him:

> Everyone who hears these words of mine and puts them into practice is like a wise man who built his house on the rock. The rain came down, the streams rose, and the winds blew and beat against that house; yet it did not fall, because it had its foundation on the rock. But everyone who hears

these words of mine and does not put them into practice is like a foolish man who built his house on sand. The rain came down, the streams rose, and the winds blew and beat against that house, and it fell with a great crash. (Matt. 7:24–27)

In this teaching, He praised the wise builder for establishing his house on the rock. He said that this person is the one who "hears these words of mine and puts them into practice." Don't miss the last part of that sentence: the one who "puts them into practice" is deemed wise.

Standing upon the Solid Rock is more than just an intellectual belief that He is our Redeemer. There is also a commitment to live out His teachings. Jesus calls us to plant our feet on His Word and stand firm in His truth.

In the modern-day church, there seems to be a huge disconnect between believing in Jesus and obeying Him. Many people readily confess Jesus as Savior, but those who live according to His words are few and far between. As a result, we fail to experience the fullness of the abundant life. We don't witness the overflow, as Peter did, of what happens when we take Jesus at His word.

When we obey Jesus, we testify with our lives that we believe Him and love Him. Obedience is the heart response of those who have been redeemed by the grace of God. Not only is this our right reaction to grace, but it also proves to be our ultimate protection and blessing in life.

One important concept for us to understand is the biblical meaning of the word *hear*. In the Bible, the term used for "hear" is the same as "obey." This word is *shema*, which means to hear and to act. There was never a distinction between hearing God's words and obeying His words. Peter responded in obedience when Jesus told him to put the boat back in the water and let down the nets. The proof that Peter heard Jesus was his response to Him. Parents can easily comprehend this concept. We instruct our kids to clean up their rooms, only to walk in an hour later and find a complete mess. We respond by saying, "Did you not hear me?" The reason we ask this question is that action was not taken. The child did not obey what was heard.

We can't just hear Christ's teachings and not follow through with action. Not only is obedience the proof that we love Him, but obedience also protects us from calamity, shields us from the destructive consequences of sin, and establishes our lives on a foundation of truth. I recently read a powerful example of how one builder, who faithfully followed commands, was spared utter destruction.

> In 1992, Hurricane Andrew destroyed thousands of homes in South Florida. Yet in an area where the wreckage looked like a war zone, one house remained *standing, still firmly anchored to its foundation*. When a reporter asked the homeowner why his house had not been blown away, he replied, "I built this house myself. I also built it according to the Florida state building code. When the code called for 2" x 6" roof trusses, I used 2" x 6" roof trusses. I was told that a house built according to code could withstand a hurricane—and it did" (emphasis added).[1]

Don't miss this crucial testimony! The one house that remained standing was the one built by a man who carefully followed the building codes of the experts. These were not merely suggestions; they were vital to survival. Jesus never expected us to simply sit in churches or listen to podcasts to learn about Him. No, He expects us to build our lives upon His words. When we do, our lives will stand against the storms of life.

Just as the Florida state building codes were absolute and required for a home to withstand a hurricane, so God's Word is necessary for us to stand. Although culture will shift and sway over time and what is considered good and right will rise and fall with the whims of the world, God's truth is unchanging.

Your statutes, LORD, stand firm. (Ps. 93:5)

All his precepts are trustworthy.
They are established forever and ever. (111:7–8)

The grass withers and the flowers fade,
   but the word of our God stands forever.
   (Isa. 40:8 NLT)

It is God alone who establishes what is good and right for the soul. His commandments are much like guardrails that keep us from driving off cliffs. If we ignore them and barrel past the protection, we end up in destruction. His truth is absolute; it is not relative. When we build our lives upon His principles, we are blessed; if we ignore His instructions, we face devastating consequences.

We live in a day and age when many are offended at the mention of absolute truth. But God—not men and women or government systems—is who determines what is right and wrong. The One who created the world and all that is in it is the One who knows how it best operates. When we align ourselves with His Word, we are like the builder who followed the codes and was able to withstand a hurricane.

Culture's values will change, and we will be tempted to conform. But we must be unwavering in our biblical convictions concerning the sanctity of human life, God's design for marriage, the sacredness of sex, the importance of truth and integrity, the scourge of racism, and our Christian call to stand up for the oppressed. As Christ followers, our values will be different from the world's, but we must always remain loving toward those who disagree with us.

Obedience to God's commands provides the strongest foundation for us to stand upon. We must be aware that the Enemy loves to distort what is right and true so that he can weaken our position of victory. Therefore, one of the greatest problems the church faces today is not the pressure of the world to conform; instead, it is the false teachers within the church, who undermine God's Word and teach others to ignore His loving commands.

The Bible clearly warns us that we must stand firm against those who teach things that do not align with God's truth. Although these teachers may be popular and sound loving, we must use our discernment to discover the harm in the message.

If we as Christ followers are going to obey God and stand firm in the midst of cultural pressures to conform to ungodliness, we must recognize the deceptive and lying voices that tempt us to ignore His commands. One of the signs of the end times is an increase of false teachers in the church: "The time will come when people will not put up with sound doctrine. Instead, to suit their own desires, they will gather around them a great number of teachers to say what their itching ears want to hear. They will turn their ears away from the truth and turn aside to myths" (2 Tim. 4:3–4).

Imagine a world in which physicians tell patients that the cancerous tumors in their bodies are actually good and should be celebrated. Instead of addressing the sickness that is killing the patients, the physicians ignore it and send away the patients with a false sense of security for the future. The doctors' lies are easy to believe because the patients would much rather hear positive messages than negative ones, even if the negative ones ultimately result in healing. But millions would die if this kind of treatment were tolerated in the medical profession.

Visualize in the same scenario that there are doctors who, out of genuine love for their patients, speak the truth. Even though it may be initially hard to hear, these doctors feel an obligation to clearly diagnose the tumors and give clear courses of treatment. These doctors want to see their patients whole and alive. Yet shockingly, in this bizarre world, the doctors who speak truth are labeled unloving, while the ones who speak lies are considered good.

Friends, this is the jacked-up world we live in.

Our culture celebrates what God says is destructive to our bodies, minds, souls, and spirits. And there are many teachers in the church who either endorse or ignore a lifestyle of sin that ultimately destroys the soul. We must be careful and discerning. Not everything that sounds loving and kind is actually either.

The most loving thing Jesus does for us is convict us of sin, helping us turn from it and experience healing. He is the Great Physician! He doesn't ignore our brokenness; He calls our attention to it because He desires our wholeness. He knows that all sin leads to death, and He wants us to experience real life in Him. When we gravitate toward those who teach us what our ears want to hear instead of what is good for our souls, we remain stuck in our sin and sickness.

In order for us to stand firm, we must plant our feet firmly in the absolute truth of God's Word. We can't pick and choose based on what is approved by the culture. Sure, this stance might not be popular, but we must come to the place where we are more concerned with being right with God than being right with man. Plus, there are incredible blessings to those who hold fast to God's Word. The apostle James stated it this way:

> Do not merely listen to the word, and so deceive yourselves. Do what it says. Anyone who listens to the word but does not do what it says is like someone who looks at his face in a mirror and, after looking at himself, goes away and immediately forgets what he looks like. But whoever looks intently into the perfect law that gives freedom, and continues in it—not forgetting what they have heard, but doing it—they will be blessed in what they do. (James 1:22–25)

What is the result of obedience? The Bible is clear that there are blessings—tremendous blessings—to the one who obeys God's Word.

But the opposite is also true. When we ignore God's commandments and walk in disobedience, we reap harvests of destruction.

THE ABUNDANT LIFE

God's commandments are not merely rules to follow; they prove a pathway to blessing. As we've noted, obedience does not earn our salvation, but it is the legitimate response to God's love and grace. When we put His precepts into practice and obey His truths, we declare with our lives that we believe Him and trust Him. According to biblical scholar and theologian W. E. Vines, "Faith is of the heart, invisible to men; obedience is of the conduct and may be observed. When a man obeys God he gives the only possible evidence that in his heart he believes God."[2]

I'll never forget discovering the "love + faith = obedience" formula when I was a new believer. As I've shared, my life before Jesus was filled with sin and destruction. I saw obedience to God as a burden and something I "had to do." But after I experienced God's love and grace, my heart changed. The Holy Spirit took up residence in my heart, and I wanted more than anything else in the world to live for His glory and align my life with His truth. His teachings weren't mere rules to follow—far from it! God's words became my protection and delight.

I wanted to follow Him because I trusted His heart. I wanted to build my life upon His words because I believed He is good. I wanted to obey Him because I loved Him.

I am living proof that blessings come from obedience. God's Word is right, and when we live according to it, we experience His favor and goodness. My before-and-after-Jesus transformation is proof that His words bring life and blessing to the soul.

Now, don't get me wrong. I've walked through many seasons of suffering, temptation, trials, and testing. Jesus warned that storms will strike both the wise and the foolish, but the difference proves that those who build upon the Rock stand firm.

Even as a Christ follower, I've faced seasons of temptation to doubt God's Word and not live according to His truth. Back when I was still single, I was tempted to disobey God and walk in the ways of the world concerning sex and relationships. But something in my heart said that Jesus is better. Instead of settling for the world's version of love and sex, I trusted God and waited for His best. My words fail to express how richly God blessed me because of this one choice of obedience. Avoiding sexual sin spared me tremendous heartbreak and also paved the way for a beautiful marriage.

Please don't hear this as bragging. I'm just a sister in Christ begging others to do the same. I'm boasting in the grace of God and the blessings that come from obedience. I've tasted and seen that the Lord is good, and my heart burns for others to take Him at His word.

> Whoever scorns instruction will pay for it,
> but whoever respects a command is rewarded.
> (Prov. 13:13)

> Blessed … are those who hear the word of God and
> obey it. (Luke 11:28)

Just yesterday I received a devastating message from a young woman who walked away from God after college. She's been living a lifestyle of sin, even though she knew better. She did not build her life on Jesus's words, and now she is in shambles. She's in a dating relation-ship with a man who is emotionally and physically abusive. She feels stuck with him because of the sexual bond and can't break free. She just discovered she is pregnant, and this guy is forcing her to have an abortion. She's miserable. She's scared. She's searching for help.

My heart breaks for her, and I am standing with her in this storm, helping her plant her feet on the Rock again. But as I survey the damage done, I wonder what would have happened if she had trusted God and obeyed Him. What if she had rejected the world's ways concerning sex and relationships? How much misery would this young woman have been spared if she had believed God?

God is good! His commandments are not intended to hinder our pleasure but rather to protect us. Sin lies and steals; Jesus protects and heals. Whether it is God's teachings concerning forgiveness, finances, marriage, gluttony, or anger, all His commandments prove beneficial and a blessing to the ones who build their lives upon them.

One thing we must always keep in mind is this: love is always the motivation for obedience. After all, God desires our hearts. He wants relationships, not robots. Jesus said it this way: "You are my friends if you do what I command" (John 15:14). He's not seeking our blind obedience to a set of rules. The Lord seeks men and women who are enchanted with Him and long to please their Redeemer.

Our relationships with God are lived out through His Holy Spirit, who indwells us. The Spirit of God has one thing on His agenda: to glorify God. He longs to please the Father and show the world that Jesus is better. When we obey His voice (which is God's Word written on our hearts), we are in right relationship with God. Because we have free will, we still have a choice to obey the Spirit and live in a way that honors the Lord or to follow our sinful nature and live outside His will.

Notice how Ephesians teaches us to "put off" disobedient actions so that we don't hinder our intimacy with God:

> Each of you must put off falsehood and speak truthfully to your neighbor, for we are all members of one body. "In your anger do not sin": Do not let the sun go down while you are still angry, and do not give the devil a foothold. Anyone who has been stealing must steal no longer, but must work, doing something useful with their own hands, that they may have something to share with those in need.
>
> Do not let any unwholesome talk come out of your mouths, but only what is helpful for building others up according to their needs, that it may benefit those who listen. And do not grieve the Holy Spirit of God, with whom you were sealed for the day of redemption. Get rid of all bitterness, rage and anger, brawling and slander, along with every form of malice. (Eph. 4:25–31)

In this passage, we see a long list of sinful actions. Anger, rage, gossip, stealing, lying—all of these are examples of disobedience to God's Word. The Holy Spirit living in us wants to please God and obey His Word. Therefore, when we ignore His voice and continue in these sins, the Bible says we "grieve" the Spirit.

ALL OTHER GROUND IS SINKING SAND

To grieve the Spirit does not mean we lose our salvation, but it does mean we lose our fellowship with Him until we repent. Remember, this fellowship is God's primary desire; this is why He redeemed us in the first place. When we disobey the Spirit, our hearts become hardened and we don't experience the overflow of blessings.

Here is the good news for anyone currently living in the consequences of sin: you can start fresh; you can stand! Repentance simply means we turn away from our sin and turn back to Jesus. Repentance is confessing the wrong, asking forgiveness, and accepting anew the grace of God. When we agree with God about our sin, our intimacy with the Spirit is restored and we can walk in fellowship again.

Our God is a great Redeemer. I shared with my new friend who is living in sexual sin the story of the prodigal son. I said, "Sweet girl, run home! Jesus will welcome you with open arms, and He can transform this mess. You can start fresh today. You can trust God, obey His truths, and experience the joyful, abundant life promised by Christ Himself."

As we've seen in previous chapters, each principle we learn prepares us for the many times we'll be forced to stand against darkness, temptation, and persecution. For the Christ follower, it is imperative that we stand firmly on God's Word and build our lives on the solid foundation of truth. Otherwise, we leave ourselves wide open to the destructive forces of the Evil One, which we will learn more about in the next section.

The choice is ours. Will we be wise or foolish? Will we stand on the Rock or on sinking sand?

Friends, choose today to rise up and plant your feet on the Solid Rock. Allow His grace to flood your heart. Remain steadfast as a beloved child robed in righteousness. Live entirely out of a heart that experiences His extravagant love and responds with full surrender and obedience. Take steps of obedience, and I promise that you will experience God's goodness like never before.

Just as Peter had to respond in obedience to Jesus's words before he experienced the miraculous catch of fish, we must respond to Jesus's commands before we see how they will transform our lives. I'm sure Peter had absolutely no clue that the greatest catch of his life awaited him when he shoved his boat back into the water the morning he encountered Jesus. Yet Peter experienced firsthand the abundant blessings that come from obedience. His boat literally overflowed with evidence. I imagine that the next time Jesus asked Peter to go fishing, he didn't put up any arguments. Your first step may be difficult, but let me encourage you with this truth: His grace will meet you there and enable you to walk in His ways.

This truth I also know from experience: Jesus is better! Life is empty without Him, and we can withstand the storms of life only with Him, so let's choose today to plant our feet on the Solid Rock and stand firm in His truth!

STAND

· · · · · · · · · ·

THE POSITION OF VICTORY

Put on the full armor of God, so that when the day of
evil comes, you may be able to stand your ground.

Ephesians 6:13

Chapter 6

· · · · · · ·

STAND FIRM AGAINST THE WAVES

When the storm has swept by, the wicked are gone,
but the righteous stand firm forever.

Proverbs 10:25

With toes burrowed deep into the sand and legs planted in a firm stance, my whole body was securely balanced and braced for the impact. After several rounds of defeat against the mighty waves, this time, I stood ready for the onslaught as they pounded against me. Wave after wave, my instincts grew stronger and my response more adept as I learned to stand firm.

Vacationing at the beach is always good for my soul. I love nothing more than the sound of the tide rolling in and the smell of sea air. Last summer I spent a few days with my family enjoying the white sand and crystal-blue water of Seaside, Florida. In my opinion, the stretch of coast known as 30A boasts some of the most beautiful beaches in the world. And have I mentioned that they serve frozen key-lime pie on a stick? There are no words.

Normally I'm content to sit by the shore as the waves roll in, lounging under an umbrella with nothing but a good beach read in hand. The beach is where I rest. My typical agenda is all about relaxation, but it wasn't going to happen.

On that particular day, our youngest son, Brenden, wanted to body surf. The name aptly describes this activity. The surfer wades into the water and waits on the board for the wave to crest. He then paddles his guts out to catch the wave and enjoys the thrill of riding it to shore. Bustling with energy, Brenden had a very different beach agenda from my own. His boyish enthusiasm could not be contained. My husband was busy with a last-minute work project. I was left as the parental lifeguard. On a typical summer day, this would be no big deal, but there was a storm warning, and the waters were especially rough and too dangerous for a little boy to maneuver alone.

Looking up from my book, I saw that he was being carried away by the current and was struggling against the waves. Concerned for his safety, I rushed out into warm water. Just a few yards into the sea, I felt the intense crush of water pound against me. The waves pounding against me were powerful—so strong, in fact, that I found myself knocked over and sucking salt water up my nose with the first swell.

The force had taken me by surprise. So much for not getting my hair wet. Sputtering and flailing about, I was soaked and blowing salt water out of my nose like a porpoise. With pound after pound, the waves sent me backward. Finally, I reached Brenden, and we were both pulled under by a huge crashing wave. After a few trips under and more ocean water in my mouth than is healthy for the human body, I determined then and there that we were in danger and I needed to learn to stand.

Standing is part mental, part physical. There is a preparation of mind and will that informs muscles and tendons. Standing is a decision of the will before it is a positional reality. Gripping Brenden's hand, I rose to my feet, braced my legs, dug my toes into the sand, shifted my weight, and prepared for the next impact. That time, as I watched the wave swell and crest in front of me, I was ready for it and able to stand firm.

Life for a Christ follower can feel much like standing against crashing waves. But the ones we face are not made of water; rather, they are often mental and emotional attacks against our hearts and minds. We often face waves of doubt and fear, or we get knocked over by depression and anxiety. We get dragged down by a riptide of insecurity and shame. Dismayed, we scramble to our feet, puzzled at our weak faith, only to get knocked down again before we know what hit us. Many Christ followers feel shame and defeat in the midst of these struggles, not realizing they are under spiritual attack or that we can experience victory. Here's what pastor and author Chip Ingram says about the topic:

> There are many, many reasons for depression and discouragement—medical, chemical, psychological, social, and the like—but when dark moments strike out of the blue for no apparent reason, it should sound an alarm. One minute you're thinking about how well things are going and the next you're on a

downward spiral of negative thoughts. Why? Because there are invisible realities that have everything to do with whether you experience the abundant life that Jesus promised, serve fruitfully in God's kingdom, and know the joy of your salvation.[1]

I'm going to shoot straight with you: we live in a war zone. This world is not neutral. We have a spiritual Enemy who seeks to "steal and kill and destroy" (John 10:10). But the good news is rooted in the gospel. Jesus triumphed over Satan at the cross. He "rescued us from the dominion of darkness" (Col. 1:13) and transferred us to the kingdom of God. We are now seated victoriously with Christ. We don't fight for victory but rather from a place of victory. Knowing the difference is a game changer.

Although the war was won, the battle still rages. Satan is a defeated foe, yet he still wages his demonic assaults. His murderous rage, fueled by jealousy of the Most High, is aimed at the redeemed image bearers of the one true God. The apostle Peter warned us of this reality: "Be alert and of sober mind. Your enemy the devil prowls around like a roaring lion looking for someone to devour" (1 Pet. 5:8).

To stand firm, we must be alert to the battle.

The sad fact remains that many Christians are ignorant of Satan's schemes. I know I have been far too many times. We assume the waves that knock us down time and time again are just our own thoughts, fears, weaknesses, and emotions. If we are to stand firm in this day, we must wise up to the various assaults that seek to topple us.

In the book of Ephesians, the apostle Paul taught us about our victorious position in Christ as children of God. The first half of the epistle focuses on the realities of our salvation and what Christ accomplished for us on the cross. The second half teaches us how to walk out our status as redeemed children of God. In the final chapter, we are taught to "stand firm" in our victorious position.

> Be strong in the Lord and in his mighty power. Put on the full armor of God, so that you can *take your stand* against the devil's schemes. For our struggle is not against flesh and blood, but against the rulers, against the authorities, against the powers of this dark world and against the spiritual forces of evil in the heavenly realms. Therefore put on the full armor of God, so that when the day of evil comes, you may be *able to stand* your ground, and after you have done everything, to *stand. Stand firm.* (Eph. 6:10–14)

Notice a few key points from this passage: First, we are called to be "strong" in Jesus's mighty power. As Christ followers, we aren't victims to the Enemy's attacks; we are equipped to stand. Jesus's mighty power is within us, and the Word of God declares that "the one who is in you is greater than the one who is in the world" (1 John 4:4). It is imperative we understand it is only in the name of Jesus and in His power that we can stand against the evil that oppresses us. Next, notice the text does not say *if* the day of evil comes but *when* the day of evil comes. Spiritual warfare is a reality all believers will face. Therefore, if we are to experience victory in this life, we must learn to stand.

WHEN THE DAY OF EVIL COMES

It is vital for your survival as a Christian that you realize that when you became a Christian, you were drafted into God's army. Daily you are engaged in a battle with an unseen spiritual enemy that seeks to destroy you. Otherwise, when trials hit, you will think that something is wrong. You will wonder why God has allowed this. You won't understand the reality of your situation.[2]

It's one thing to acknowledge the fact that spiritual warfare exists, but how do we know when we are in the midst of it? What does this battle look and feel like? Although I've heard of and experienced some physical manifestations from it, for the vast majority of us, the battle the Enemy rages is against our minds. He does this through deception, accusation, temptation, and condemnation, just to name a few methods. For instance, when Satan went after Adam and Eve in the garden of Eden, he didn't use blunt force. He used words, just as he does with us today:

- Words of shame that heap condemnation on our hearts
- Words of fear that whisper dreadful scenarios
- Words of accusation that divide relationships

- Words of judgment that cause self-hatred and self-harm
- Words of doubt that lead us to question God and His Word

These assaults can at times feel like a fog, thick with despair and eclipsing joy, peace, and purpose. I've also heard some describe it as a cloud, dense and foreboding, that blocks light and joy. Others describe a weight sitting on their chests that lingers and won't lift. This battle can be described using many metaphors and emotions, but the key point to recognize is the mental and emotional nature of the attack and how specifically crafted each message is to the recipient.

Our Enemy is not all-knowing or all-powerful, but he is extremely cunning and creates chaos unique to the individual. Just as a lion stalks prey, looking for weaknesses, our Enemy observes us and sees opportunities and vulnerabilities.

Recently I took to social media to find out if I'm alone in my struggles and insecurities. Friends and strangers from far and wide bravely shared their experiences with spiritual warfare. For example, some struggle with intense feelings of insecurity or unworthiness when under attack, which is different from your run-of-the-mill low self-esteem. These assaults are ruthless and highly personal and condemning in nature. One woman who loves God but from time-to-time is flooded with shameful images from her past told of a voice that taunts her with memories from her former life, keeping her bowed down in shame. How does this woman who is forgiven stand firm in Christ's finished work when the voice of shame screams?

Another friend struggles with the lies of perfectionism. The voice taunts her with the thought that she must be perfect to be loved. Thinner. Younger. Prettier. Waves of accusation hit her with lies about her worth. Comparison. Self-hatred. Self-harm. She feels unlovable unless she conforms to a subjective image of perfection. The accusations lead to dangerous and damaging choices. She knows in her heart that these accusations are lies, yet she doesn't know how to stand against them.

Another man shared that he is bombarded by a voice of intimidation. He is a man of God, called to ministry, yet he often endures oppressive thoughts that try to silence his witness. He described the attack as a threatening voice that whispers warnings against standing up boldly in his faith. "Don't share the gospel." "You'll be laughed right out of here if you say that you believe the Bible." "Don't speak the name of Jesus." Taunts like these intimidate him not to stand for Christ. By harnessing the fear of rejection and persecution, the voice paralyzes his ministry and hinders him from boldly proclaiming his faith. How does this man remain steadfast in the midst of intimidation?

Another friend is consistently overwhelmed with fear, her mind a theater that projects dangers, dread, and darkness. Instead of walking by faith and trusting God with her future, she is flooded with worry and anxiety as her mind entertains what-if scenarios. Her mind is a battlefield. She knows Scripture and can teach others truth, but when the waves of fear strike, she's knocked down. She hates her lack of faith and then feels condemned for giving in to fear. How can she stand against such a powerful emotion?

And lest we forget one of the biggest of the waves that seek to take us out: doubt. It strikes as a tsunami to the soul. Men and women, young and old, describe the mental assault of doubt that sabotages us with lies about God's character, existence, and goodness. What is common in each of these testimonies is that the doubts completely contradict what the individuals truly believe. They are puzzled. "Where do these thoughts come from?" "Am I not a Christian?" "These can't be my thoughts. I love and trust God. I don't know why I'm struggling with doubt."

Isn't it nice to feel that you're not alone? When I read story after story of such similar experiences, I knew that these were not just coincidences but intentional warfare.

What all of these situations have in common is the author. The mastermind behind the madness is the one whom Jesus called the "father of lies" (John 8:44). Just as he brought about the first sin through deception (see Gen. 3), still today his mode of operation is to infiltrate our lives by influencing our thoughts. And as the apostle Paul said to the Corinthians, "I am afraid that just as Eve was deceived by the serpent's cunning, your minds may somehow be led astray from your sincere and pure devotion to Christ" (2 Cor. 11:3).

Don't miss this: Paul warned us that our "minds" can be "led astray." This is Satan's specialty, and we see this truth depicted in the names he is known by in Scripture. Each title gives us insight into his ways:

- Adversary (see 1 Thess. 2:18 YLT)
- Slanderer (see 1 Pet. 5:8)
- Tempter (see 1 Thess. 3:5)
- Liar (see John 8:44)
- Accuser (see Rev. 12:10)

Perhaps you're reading this and thinking, *I'd rather not contemplate the Enemy, thank you very much.* I get that, but here's the thing: the Enemy has ground to infiltrate our lives only through our lack of knowledge. He was defeated at the cross. His only weapons are lies and deception. If we are to stand firm, we must know who and what seek to defeat us.

Any coach preparing for a big game or any military commander preparing troops for battle will take time to study the opponent. We don't want to be people who are overly focused on the Enemy, but we must absolutely be equipped for battle. The more we recognize who he is, how he operates, and our position of victory, the more fully we are prepared to resist him.

Concerning the schemes of the Enemy, Chip Ingram wrote this:

> [Satan's schemes] are orchestrated in order to tempt us, deceive us, draw us away from God, fill our hearts with half-truths and untruths, and lure us into pursuing good things in the wrong way, at the wrong time, or with the wrong person. The English word *strategies* is derived from the Greek word Paul uses that is translated "schemes." That means our temptations are not random. The false perspectives we encounter do not come at us haphazardly. The lies we hear, the conflicts we have with others, the cravings that consume us when we are at our weakest points—they are all part of a plan to make us casualties in the invisible war. They are organized,

below-the-belt assaults designed to neutralize the very people God has filled with his awesome power.[3]

Spiritual warfare comes in many forms and proves unique to each individual. Here are some of the various waves or mental assaults the Enemy employs through demonic spirits that oppose us:

- Deception—worldly philosophies that contradict God's truth and take us captive
- Intimidation—overt pressure to silence a Christ follower from being bold in the faith or sharing the gospel
- Distraction—the daily noise and interruptions that keep a Christ follower from reading the Bible, praying, and serving God
- Temptation—rationalization and thoughts that seek to justify sin and rebellion, undermining the goodness of God and questioning the authority of His Word
- Seduction—intense pull toward ungodliness that lures Christians away from God
- Condemnation—shame and guilt heaped upon the Christian who falls into sin combined with the thought that forgiveness is not available
- Accusation—negative suggestions, speculations, and projections about you, others, or God, which divide and destroy fellowship

Although this list is depressing, I have encouraging news: we can stand against each of these! Yes, the waves will strike, but God's Word teaches us how to stand firm. The key to resisting Satan's schemes is found in 2 Corinthians 1:21–22, which says, "It is God who makes both us and you stand firm in Christ. He anointed us, set his seal of ownership on us, and put his Spirit in our hearts as a deposit, guaranteeing what is to come."

Three things are highlighted in this verse that we must take to heart:

- God equips us to stand firm.
- He set His "seal of ownership on us," declaring that we belong to Him!
- God placed His Holy Spirit in us. The Bible tells us that greater is He who is in us than he who is in this world (see 1 John 4:4)!

How do we stand in the face of these beating waves? By planting our feet firmly in our identity in Christ. Our position as beloved children of God gives us victory over the Evil One. The moment we placed faith in Jesus, we were rescued from the domain of darkness and positioned triumphantly with Christ. The more we comprehend this truth and believe it, standing firm in this reality, the more we will experience victory over the darkness. As we will discover in future chapters, our identity in Christ is intrinsically connected to the armor of God we are equipped with for battle.

To illustrate, let me share an experience that taught me how to stand against the powerful waves of accusation and condemnation.

FROM DECEPTION TO DECLARATION

The waves of accusations crashing against my mind began something like this: *No one loves you. You don't have even one true friend who cares about you. You are unwanted; you always have been, and you always will be. The world would be better off if you were dead.*

The waves of this particular mental attack began to hit about three weeks prior to a conference my ministry hosts for women. Every year we experience various attacks leading up to this event. I'm accustomed to the typical annoyances, such as cars breaking down, logistical setbacks, and random illnesses. But this summer, the battle was so sinister that I didn't realize I was under attack until it engulfed me.

I got hit by wave after wave of rejection. By rejection, I mean immense feelings of being unwanted and unloved. Irrational thoughts plagued my heart and mind that didn't have a basis in reality. These voices seemed real and wouldn't leave for weeks on end.

The condemnation began as a gentle ripple, but it grew into a massive swell that left me sobbing hot tears on my bedroom floor. The words *No one loves you* ripped through my heart and echoed in my mind as the days grew closer to the event. As much as I tried to resist, I could not stand against these lies. I simply could not believe the truth. My mind swirled with accusations, and my heart was engulfed with the searing pain of rejection. I couldn't believe or receive love from God or anyone else. My mind was bombarded with the voice continuously.

As I said before, the Enemy knows our weak spots. This particular attack was not a new tactic. As a little girl, this was the biggest lie I believed about myself. Due to a variety of wounds from my childhood, a lie formed around my heart that I was unloved. But as a grown woman, I experienced the deep love of Jesus and walked through an intense time of healing from my past wounds. The love of God transformed my life, setting me free from the past and the lies of the Enemy. I was a new creation. Without a doubt, I knew I was the beloved of God and lived in this identity for many years. I walked in freedom from insecurity and rejection. But then, even though I didn't realize it at the time, I let my guard down and was not standing firm against the Enemy's schemes.

To say this mental onslaught came out of the blue is an understatement. At the time, I was blessed with an incredible family, strong friendships, and the sweetest marriage. When the tsunami hit, I could not be reasoned with; I felt completely unloved and unwanted. My whole identity was under attack.

My heart brimmed with a pain that would not relent. Satan's fiery darts ripped through me, and every relationship was tainted with his sick suggestions. I felt rejection at every turn, most of which made no sense whatsoever. My mind was so clouded that I couldn't see clearly. Let's just say that I didn't stand firm. I fell for every dark and sinister accusation.

If I had been counseling someone else experiencing these types of negative thoughts, I would have instantly recognized it as an attack and prayed for the individual. But in the midst of it myself, I couldn't discern that my thoughts were lies and not based in reality. That's the thing about deception: we don't easily recognize that we are being deceived. My fears seemed so real, especially when random circumstances appeared to validate and point to the veracity of the taunts. For example, I would accidentally be left off an invitation list, or a close friend would forget to call me back, or my sweet husband would make a simple remark that I would completely misinterpret. I'd overhear my team whispering about something, and the voice would convince me it was about me. Crazy junk.

Wave after wave, lie after lie, the accusations pounded against my heart. Trust me, it is very hard to prepare Bible studies and minister to others when you don't want to even get out of bed. Not to sound dramatic, but at times the voice whispered that the world would be better if I didn't exist.

As the conference finally began, the attack only escalated until I was crying alone in the shower so no one else would hear me. My mind was a battlefield. And while I was fighting this intense spiritual battle, I was trying to teach others God's Word and lead this conference. Then, on the second night, I experienced a profound breakthrough that left me forever changed. As we entered into evening worship, we sang many familiar songs of praise. There is nothing in the world like worship to break the power of the Enemy. He hates it when Jesus is lifted high.

That night, the presence of God was very evident in worship. Then my friend began to sing "Good Good Father." In case you don't know this song, the profoundly simple chorus proclaims the goodness of God and our identity as His beloved children:

> You're a good, good Father
> It's who You are.
> And I'm loved by You
> It's who I am.[4]

As she led us in the song, the room broke out in praise and the Spirit of God moved. I sang these words as though my life depended on it, proclaiming truth from my heart.

I proclaimed my true identity in Christ. I proclaimed God's love for me. I proclaimed God's goodness.

As we worshipped, I felt God's love for me as His beloved daughter. The more I experienced it, the more I felt my mind, body, will, and emotions take their stand against the lies of the Evil One. The darkness covering me began to disperse, and I could see the Light!

- Truth defeats deception.
- Worship sends the Enemy running.

Declaring the truth of my identity in Christ broke the power of the Evil One over my mind. The storm clouds lifted, and I experienced freedom from the Accuser for the first time in weeks. Where my heart had known only rejection and condemnation, I experienced the deep love of God and the assurance that I was His beloved. The power of the Enemy to deceive and harass me ceased as I lifted high the goodness of God and proclaimed with authority my position as His child. I stood, arms held high, feet firmly planted in the love of the Father.

WORSHIP WINS THE WAR

There is a story in the Old Testament that illustrates the dynamic power of truth and worship to defeat our Enemy. Jehoshaphat was king of Judah when the nation was faced with a vast army threatening to destroy the inhabitants. Outnumbered and overpowered, the people of God were certain of defeat. In the face of this utter destruction, King Jehoshaphat took the matter before the Lord in prayer. I bet you can guess what happened next: God gave him the battle strategy to stand and see.

> You will not have to fight this battle. Take up your positions; stand firm and see the deliverance the LORD will give you, Judah and Jerusalem. Do not be afraid; do not be discouraged. Go out to face them tomorrow, and the LORD will be with you. (2 Chron. 20:17)

What happens next is one of the most awesome, kick-tail moments in all of Scripture. The Lord tells His people to stand and see how He alone will defeat the vast armies arrayed before them. Read the conclusion of this story carefully and note what the people of God did as the Lord fought their battle.

> He said: "Listen, King Jehoshaphat and all who live in Judah and Jerusalem! This is what the LORD says to you: 'Do not be afraid or discouraged because of this vast army. For the battle is not yours, but God's. Tomorrow march down against them. They will be climbing up by the Pass of Ziz, and you will find them at the end of the gorge in the Desert of Jeruel. *You will not have to fight this battle.* Take up your positions; stand firm and see the deliverance

the LORD will give you, Judah and Jerusalem. Do not be afraid; do not be discouraged. Go out to face them tomorrow, and the LORD will be with you.'"

Jehoshaphat bowed down with his face to the ground, and all the people of Judah and Jerusalem fell down in worship before the LORD. Then some Levites from the Kohathites and Korahites stood up and praised the LORD, the God of Israel, with a very loud voice.

Early in the morning they left for the Desert of Tekoa. As they set out, Jehoshaphat stood and said, "Listen to me, Judah and people of Jerusalem! Have faith in the LORD your God and you will be upheld; have faith in his prophets and you will be successful." After consulting the people, Jehoshaphat appointed men to sing to the LORD and to praise him for the splendor of his holiness as they went out at the head of the army, saying:

> *"Give thanks to the LORD,*
> *for his love endures forever."*

As they began to sing and praise, the LORD set ambushes against the men of Ammon and Moab and Mount Seir who were invading Judah, and they were defeated. The Ammonites and Moabites rose up against the men from Mount Seir to destroy and annihilate them. After they finished slaughtering the men from Seir, they helped to destroy one another.

When the men of Judah came to the place that overlooks the desert and looked toward the vast army, they saw only dead bodies lying on the ground; *no one had escaped.* So Jehoshaphat and his men went to carry off their plunder, and they found among them a great amount of equipment and clothing and also articles of value—more than they could take away. There was so much plunder that it took three days to collect it. *On the fourth day they assembled in the Valley of Berakah, where they praised the LORD. This is why it is called the Valley of Berakah to this day.* (2 Chron. 20:15–26)

STAND + WORSHIP = VICTORY

I have no idea how long that emotionally painful attack would have continued in my life had I not discovered the power of standing firm and proclaiming God's praise in the face of attack. Friends, victory is found in Christ alone. He fights for us. Our job is to stand and proclaim His praise. I can tell you one thing for certain: Satan and his minions will not stick around when we lift up God in worship. Nothing sends the Enemy running faster than truth proclaimed as we worship our good, good Father!

In the upcoming chapters, we will discover specific and practical ways we can stand firm against spiritual warfare. We will learn to take up the full armor of God so that we can stand victorious against Satan's schemes. As we unpack each piece of the armor, we will discover how understanding our righteousness and redeemed position as children of God equips us to resist and stand against the Evil One.

Chapter 7

. . . .

EQUIPPED FOR VICTORY

*Get up and stand on your feet. I have appeared to you to appoint you
as a servant and as a witness of what you have seen and will see of me.*

Acts 26:16

Blinded by the light of glory, Saul struggled to his feet, awed by the
immense revelation that had knocked him to the ground. Prostrate
before the living God, he was transformed. Jesus Christ, the victorious
Savior, mercifully made Himself known to this former persecutor of
Christians. For us today, this would be akin to a terrorist who planned
multiple attacks on Christian churches instead coming to faith in Jesus
and becoming a pastor and evangelist. You and I know Saul today as
the apostle Paul, and he stands as our teacher and guide as we learn to
resist the Enemy and stand firm in the midst of spiritual warfare.

Leading up to Paul's road-to-Damascus experience, this fiery man
hunted Christ followers, leaving fear and dread in his wake. Hurling
his murderous threats and pursuing them far and wide, his reputation

preceded him. The book of Acts tells us that he stood by approving as Stephen, the first martyr, breathed his last breath. What a picture of God's relentless grace: this hate-filled man experienced the same love and grace that kept Stephen standing firm until the end.

It was when Paul was on the road to Damascus that he first encountered the risen Christ. His companions heard the great noise and saw the light, but he alone emerged from the encounter a new man. This moment—this life-altering, soul-searing, grace-gripping moment—forever changed him. A new man with a new name, Paul rose from that dusty ground with one truth ringing in his heart: "To me, to live is Christ" (Phil. 1:21). This same Jesus, the One he had persecuted, was truly God Almighty and the glorious Savior. Only one response was required from Paul, and that was full surrender.

The apostle Paul was a new creation. Gone was the self-righteous man of rage; he became instead the proclaimer of grace. Paul lived for one all-consuming passion: to tell the whole world about Jesus. He would point those in the deepest of darkness to the Light of the World. Passionate for the gospel, he would stand firm against those who would seek to undermine it. He didn't waver in defending righteousness based on Christ alone. Little did he know the opposition he would face when he surrendered his life to Jesus and took a stand against the darkness.

Along the way, the apostle Paul endured more hostility, persecution, beatings, betrayals, and false accusations than just about any man in history. His life is a textbook for what it means to stand against spiritual attack. From temptations to trials, from persecution to abandonment, he experienced immense earthly suffering. He knew what it meant to be rejected by his family for his faith. He knew what it felt like to have his closest friends turn their backs on him. He knew what it meant to be imprisoned for his beliefs. He knew what it meant to encounter principalities of darkness. Countless times, he was beaten until the skin on his back fell in shreds. He was stoned by a mob and left for dead. Barraged by illness and loneliness, still he pressed on. The apostle Paul was gripped by the all-surpassing worth and glory of Jesus.

Paul taught us to stand.

As a child of the eighties, I grew up on the *Rocky* films. Nothing encapsulates the spirit of that decade quite like watching Rocky Balboa in the boxing ring. My mind is flooded by images of the battered boxer down on the mat as the referee counted, "Ten, nine, eight …," and his opponent gloated, expecting a knockout. But right in the nick of time, Rocky mustered an internal resolve that refused to quit, and he rose to his feet.

Knocked down but not knocked out. This same champion spirit resided in Paul. Though the Enemy had him on the mat, there was an internal reservoir of conviction that enabled him to stand. Time and again, in the midst of trials and persecution, church divisions and personal pain, he rose up from the dust and planted his feet on the rock of Jesus Christ.

Therefore, when we read his words in the New Testament, we hear the call to stand repeated over and over again. This posture of faith is the lifelong call of a Christ follower. One passage is the most famous of all. In Ephesians 6, Paul calls Christ followers to stand against the schemes of the Devil. And he doesn't just stop there; he teaches us how.

We are wise to sit up, take note, and listen to what the apostle Paul wrote on spiritual warfare. This teaching was not advice from a mere spectator; this was a sage soldier in God's army giving a report from the front lines of battle. He knew the Enemy's schemes personally.

I know of no greater expert to teach us how to stand in the face of evil than the apostle Paul. So without further ado, let's open our hearts and ears to this redeemed servant's teachings on how to take up the full armor of God.

> Be strong in the Lord and in his mighty power. Put on the full armor of God, so that you can take your stand against the devil's schemes. For our struggle is not against flesh and blood, but against the rulers, against the authorities, against the powers of this dark world and against the spiritual forces of evil in the heavenly realms. Therefore, put on the full armor of God, so that when the day of evil comes, you may be able to stand your ground, and after you have done everything, to stand. Stand firm then, with the belt of truth buckled around your waist, with the breastplate of righteousness in place, and with your feet fitted with the readiness that comes from the gospel of peace. In addition to all this, take up the shield of faith, with which you can extinguish all the flaming arrows of the evil one. Take the helmet of salvation and the sword of the Spirit, which is the word of God. (vv. 10–17)

First, we are reminded that this battle belongs to the Lord. Just as Moses stood firm in the face of Pharaoh's army, expecting God to do the impossible, we stand firm in the face of evil in the Lord's power. Next, we are told to clothe ourselves in the full armor of God.

Our response to spiritual warfare is not a passive engagement but an active one. As believers, we are equipped with everything needed for victory, but each of us must make the choice to put on our armor.

Note that the apostle Paul divided the armor into two main sections. The first set contains the articles that a Christ follower should wear at all times: the belt of truth, breastplate of righteousness, and shoes of peace. These pieces of armor are our ongoing, daily protection against spiritual warfare, and we will examine them in this chapter. We will learn about the final three pieces—the sword of the Spirit, shield of faith, and helmet of salvation—in the next chapter. Those elements are our defensive weapons that we "take up" when battle rages.

THE BELT OF TRUTH

Paul's description of the armor begins with a piece that may seem insignificant to us today. When most of us dress, a belt is an afterthought or the last article of clothing we put on. But for the Roman solider, the belt was an essential piece because it held the entire armor together. This understanding proves imperative for us in our desire to stand firm; without the belt of truth, nothing in our lives holds together.

What, then, is the belt of truth, and why is it so essential? The word *truth* means that which conforms to an original standard. For example, whenever a teacher administers a test, there is an answer key where the correct answers are written. Therefore, whenever a student takes the test, an answer is deemed true if it corresponds to the answer on the key. Something is true if it aligns with the original. God is the author of truth. He is the creator and sustainer of life. He defines what is right and wrong; He is ultimate truth. When our lives align with His, we are secured with the belt of truth.

So what does this have to do with our ability to stand? Every human being holds a worldview, which is essentially the way a person evaluates the world around him or her. Philosophers agree that every person answers a few key questions that compose his or her worldview, and these questions correspond to what is either true, false, or subjective. As we've noted, our Enemy specializes in one thing: deception. If Satan can deceive us through philosophies, entertainment, education, media, or religion to make us see the world contrary to God's truth, then our ability to stand firm against his schemes is weakened significantly. To arm ourselves with the belt of truth, let's examine five big life questions and see how possessing a biblical worldview equips us for victory.

1. Who Is God?

Atheists, agnostics, Hindus, Mormons, Muslims, and Christians—it doesn't matter the religion or lack thereof, every person answers this question. How people answer this one forms the foundation for their lives. Truly, one's perspective of God is primary. All other issues spring from this starting point.

The biblical Christian worldview answers this question with the triune God, who is Father, Son, and Holy Spirit. We believe in a holy, loving, relational, sovereign, merciful, all-knowing, and all-powerful Creator God. This foundational truth informs all other life questions. Our ability to stand firm against the forces of darkness, deception, and temptation requires that we know God rightly.

BUCKLE UP! THIS IS WHAT GOD'S WORD SAYS:

In the beginning God created the heavens and the earth. (Gen. 1:1)

You are worthy, our Lord and God,
    to receive glory and honor and power,
for you created all things,
    and by your will they were created
    and have their being. (Rev. 4:11)

Our first line of defense against spiritual attack is a right view of God. All other views will weaken our resolve and leave us exposed to spiritual deception.

2. Who Am I?

Are we simply masses of cells without cause or purpose? Or are we a glorious creation made in the image of God? Each person's worldview answers this question. Our Enemy loves nothing more than to deceive men and women concerning their actual identity. Therefore, we must know and believe who God declares us to be in His Word. Remember, God alone is the source of truth. He alone can tell us who we are, why we are here, and how we should live. The Enemy writes another script, and when we fall for his schemes about our purpose or origin, we are deceived.

BUCKLE UP! THIS IS WHAT GOD'S WORD SAYS:

God said, "Let us make mankind in our image, in our likeness, so that they may rule over the fish in the sea and the birds in the sky, over the livestock and all the wild animals, and over all the creatures that move along the ground."

So God created mankind in his own image,
in the image of God he created them;
male and female he created them.
(Gen. 1:26–27)

Praise be to the God and Father of our Lord Jesus Christ, who has blessed us in the heavenly realms with every spiritual blessing in Christ. For he chose us in him before the creation of the world to be holy and blameless in his sight. In love he predestined us for adoption to sonship through Jesus Christ, in accordance with his pleasure and will—to the praise

of his glorious grace, which he has freely given us in
the One he loves. (Eph. 1:3–6)

It is easy to see how the Enemy can use lies about our identity to
undermine our ability to stand firm against his schemes.

3. What Is the Problem with This World?

If there is one thing that all people agree on, it is that this world is
broken. But concluding what caused this brokenness is where the agree-
ment typically ends. Biblical Christianity points to a definitive moment
in history that fractured the world and resulted in the death, disease,
destruction, and dismal state of affairs we experience. This moment is
called the fall, and it's when sin entered the world (see Gen. 3).

The cause of this fall was Satan himself. He desired to usurp
God and establish himself as God Most High. Other religions and
worldviews point to various other causes of the world's problems:
a lack of government control, education, or resources, and so on.
Bottom line: If we don't recognize the right problem, how can we
know the right solution?

BUCKLE UP! THIS IS WHAT GOD'S WORD SAYS:

All have sinned and fall short of the glory of God.
(Rom. 3:23)

[Jesus] went on: "What comes out of a person is what
defiles them. For it is from within, out of a person's
heart, that evil thoughts come—sexual immorality,

theft, murder, adultery, greed, malice, deceit, lewdness, envy, slander, arrogance and folly. All these evils come from inside and defile a person." (Mark 7:20–23)

If we are deceived about the true problem with humanity, the Enemy can easily deceive us with false solutions.

4. What Is the Solution?

How do we mend a fractured world? Politicians and people of various religions debate this question, but how one answers this forms more than just a philosophical stance; it proves the anchor for the soul. Who or what people look to for deliverance is truly their God. For the biblical Christian, there is only One who can solve humanity's greatest problem.

BUCKLE UP! THIS IS WHAT GOD'S WORD SAYS:

God so loved the world that he gave his one and only Son, that whoever believes in him shall not perish but have eternal life. For God did not send his Son into the world to condemn the world, but to save the world through him. (John 3:16–17)

The wages of sin is death, but the gift of God is eternal life in Christ Jesus our Lord. (Rom. 6:23)

Biblical Christianity provides hope for the brokenness of this world in our Savior, Jesus Christ. When sin entered the world, bringing death and destruction, God promised a Redeemer who would restore all things. Jesus is the fulfillment of that promise. He is the solution to our sin problem and the only one who can remedy the brokenness of humanity. When we believe this truth, we are born again into the family of God. Those who reject this truth are forever attempting in vain to find a solution to fix this world and their souls. These eternal truths hold our lives together and give confidence in the midst of uncertainty.

5. Where Are We Going?

The death rate is 100 percent. Every person will die. I know this fact is morbid, but we must face reality. All worldviews answer the question of what happens when we die. The materialist believes that nothing happens after death, and Eastern religions offer reincarnation as an option. The Christian message is unique in the fact that our hope hinges on the resurrection.

BUCKLE UP! THIS IS WHAT GOD'S WORD SAYS:

We must all appear before the judgment seat of Christ, so that each of us may receive what is due us for the things done while in the body, whether good or bad. (2 Cor. 5:10)

Praise be to the God and Father of our Lord Jesus Christ! In his great mercy he has given us new birth into a living hope through the resurrection of Jesus Christ from the dead. (1 Pet. 1:3)

Our hope is found in Jesus, who defeated death, conquered the grave, and will raise us up with Him one day. Resurrection is the foundation of our faith and the hope of our tomorrow. We hold fast to the fact that we will spend eternity with God. This world is not the end, and this world is not our home.

As we can see, how we answer the five big life questions determines our worldview. Just as it was essential for the Roman solider to hold his entire armor together with a belt, it proves equally important that we are held together with a biblical worldview. Just stop for a minute and think about the millions of messages we see and hear that oppose this worldview. If our foe can undermine our ability to know truth, he gains a significant foothold in our lives.

Discernment is key to victory. Discernment means we are able to distinguish truth from falsehood. Be aware of entertainment, education, media, and philosophies that espouse a worldview that contradicts God's Word. Over time these ideas seep into our consciousness and weaken our ability to stand.

THE BREASTPLATE OF RIGHTEOUSNESS

As a prisoner of Rome, the apostle Paul spent a significant amount of time chained to a Roman soldier. From this vantage point, he had an up-close look at the armor. The breastplate refers to the part of a soldier's gear that covered the vital organs (heart, lungs, kidneys), both front and back. When under fire or during hand-to-hand combat, this breastplate was essential to survival. The same holds true for our spiritual armor. The primary place our Enemy will seek to strike is the heart. God provided us an abiding protection from the Evil One: the breastplate of righteousness.

Righteousness means to have a right standing before God. Think back to the story of the prodigal son in chapter 4. When the son was welcomed back into his father's home, he was covered with a robe, which represented his being "right" with his father and welcomed into the family. This guy did nothing to deserve this acceptance; he was welcomed home completely by grace.

So how are we made right with God? There are two options. The first approach some take is to try to keep the holy Law of God perfectly; this attempt is called self-righteousness or legalism. This approach is filled with fear, striving, and hard work. Self-righteous people seek to earn their way into God's favor through good works or obedience to the Law. The problem with this method is that it's impossible to live a perfect life. We can't clean ourselves up enough to earn our way back into God's favor. Just like the prodigal son, we require grace. Therefore, we must turn to the only true option: imputed righteousness.

I know, I know, *imputed* is a big theological word. But it is a good one. *Imputed* means "something attributed to one by another." When we place faith in Jesus, a great exchange takes place. He takes away our sin, and we take on His perfect righteousness. At that point, we can stand before God clean, forgiven, and beloved. And that's not based on our works, rule keeping, or human effort; it's 100 percent because of Jesus: "God made him who had no sin to be sin for us, so that in him we might become the righteousness of God" (2 Cor. 5:21).

How does imputed righteousness protect us from the Evil One? Remember, our Enemy is also known as the "accuser of our brothers and sisters" (Rev. 12:10). He hurls accusations and calls into question our status as God's children.

Have you ever heard a voice whisper, "God could never love you for what you've done"?

Have you ever felt crippled with shame because of your past?

Have you felt as though you needed to work harder to earn God's love?

Each of these scenarios is an example of a fiery dart launched at our hearts. Left to our own devices, we would be found guilty, but when we put our faith in Christ, we are covered by His righteousness. Now the Accuser has no grounds against us. Jesus stands as our defense.

So when the Accuser points to our past and accuses us with shame and condemnation, we point to Jesus and stand firm in His finished work, His *imputed* righteousness.

There is a second aspect of righteousness that absolutely can't be passed over. If we ignore this, we leave ourselves wide open to the Enemy and his ability to harass us. This is called *practiced* righteousness, which is when, in our daily conduct and lifestyle, we choose to live obediently to God's will. As we discovered in chapter 5, we don't obey God to earn His love. Instead, obedience is our response to His love for us. When we practice righteousness, we remain in the will of God and under the protective covering of the Most High. When we choose to sin and disobey Him, we expose ourselves to the Enemy's fiery darts and arrows.

Let me illustrate how these two aspects of righteousness work in tandem. When I first trusted Christ as Savior, I was declared 100 percent righteous, but I still had a choice as to whether I would live in obedience to God. At that time, there were several open doors to the Enemy: lying, unforgiveness, and gossip, just to name a few. Because I did not practice righteousness in those areas, I experienced spiritual defeat. Therefore, Satan gained access to oppress me. Could he take away my salvation? No! But he sure could mess with my life. When I repented of these sins, I discovered not only the joy of living in God's will but also the benefit of His protective covering. Our ability to stand firm against Satan's schemes requires the full breastplate of righteousness, both imputed and practiced.

In Ephesians 4, Paul taught us how this works. In this teaching, he described our old and new natures in terms of clothing we wear. We are taught to "put off" (lay aside) the old sinful nature and "put on" the new righteous nature.

> *Put off* your old self, which belongs to your former manner of life and is corrupt through deceitful desires, and ... be renewed in the spirit of your minds, and ... *put on* the new self, created after the likeness of God in true righteousness and holiness.
>
> Therefore, having put away falsehood, let each one of you speak the truth with his neighbor, for we are members one of another. Be angry and do not sin; do not let the sun go down on your anger, and *give no opportunity to the devil.* (vv. 22–27 ESV)

Notice Paul's conclusion that we should "put off" our old sinful nature so that we "give no opportunity to the devil."

Opportunity? I know a young woman who attends church regularly, posts Scripture on social media, and claims to be a Christ follower yet lives in utter defeat and darkness. Her life does not bear the fruit or abundance that is the inheritance of a child of God. I love this young woman dearly and hurt to see her life in disarray; her finances are in shambles, her relationships are in discord, and her emotions are a roller coaster. It is not my place to judge her salvation. I will assume that because she professes Jesus, she has His righteous covering. But her life is a train wreck because she does not obey God.

She continues to live in known sin and can't understand why she doesn't experience the abundant life promised in Scripture. The sin in her life provides an opportunity for the Devil to steal her blessings. After all, Satan is a thief, and he will steal our joy, peace, relationships, finances, and marriages if we give him access.

PROTECT YOUR HEART!

Putting on the breastplate of righteousness is our spiritual protection against the fiery darts that seek to strike our hearts. When we stand firm in who we are as God's beloved children, Satan's accusations bounce right off our armor. Likewise, when we "put off" our old sinful practices and choose to live righteously, we effectively shut down the majority of Satan's opportunities to attack and we cover ourselves from unnecessary harm.

THE SHOES OF PEACE

Take it from me: a good pair of shoes is essential to stability. I remember the first time I traveled to Europe. I was with a group of girlfriends, and we decided to be adventurous and backpack. I'm not the lowest maintenance of gals, so this was quite the feat for this big-haired Texas girl. Five countries, ten days, and all of life's big essentials in a backpack. We barely slept, but, oh, did we eat! I'm pretty sure I consumed every croissant on the Continent.

By the time we finally arrived in Italy, I was ready to chuck my shoes into the Venice canals. I'd made the mistake of wearing flip-flops on our trek across Europe. Bad idea. When carrying my heavy backpack on cobblestone streets, I would slip, turn my ankle, and fall over and over again. My shoe choice was a big mistake. Those flimsy sandals did not equip me to stand and were not sufficient for the activities we faced each day.

Quality footwear is essential for our spiritual lives as well. If our feet aren't stable, our lives aren't either. I meet Jesus-loving men and women all the time who live in fear. Although they know the Lord, their emotions are ruled by dreadful anxiety. Their souls are not at rest. Why? Their feet are not securely planted in the gospel of peace, so their thoughts are tormented by all kinds of scenarios.

Friends, riding the roller coaster of worry makes us sick, which is exactly where Satan and his minions would love to keep us in bondage. Nothing pleases our Enemy more than the thought that we would live in fear instead of faith.

I heard someone once say that *fear* means "false evidence appearing real." This definition explains very well the type of warfare we endure on a daily basis. Our foe paints scenarios in our minds that project future realities and cause us to feel hopeless and defeated. But every scenario the Enemy portrays lacks the presence of God with us. Satan will never add Jesus to his equation. Although he will barrage our minds with doom, he will never include the fact that God is with us, for us, and our defender. Satan never adds the gospel to his equations. The gospel, which makes us beloved children of the heavenly Father, speaks a better word over our future than does any projection of the Evil One. Therefore, it is essential that we stand "firm-footed in the gospel of peace" (Eph. 6:15 ISV).

If you've ever played tug-of-war, you know how easy it is to be pulled to the ground or lose your balance if your feet are not planted. When a Roman soldier was pitted against an enemy in hand-to-hand combat, the one who stood until the end was the victor. For this reason, the soldiers wore sandals that wrapped tightly around the ankle and calf. The soles were fitted with sharp spikes that drove into the ground when they stood, enabling them to maintain firm footing when under attack. We must use a similar tactic against our Enemy.

LACE UP YOUR SHOES AND STAND FIRM!

What gives us sure footing when we are under attack? It is the knowledge that we are at peace with God. It is the confidence that we belong to Jesus and that no weapon formed against us will prosper. It is the peace that floods our hearts when we remember "He's got this" and nothing in this world can separate us from His love. The peace we have with God gives us the ability to resist, remain steadfast, and renounce the Evil One.

Once again, the apostle Paul unpacked for us how Jesus's finished work grants us supernatural peace. The following passage is found at the conclusion of Romans 8, where the Word of God has declared that there is no condemnation for anyone who is "in Christ

Jesus," and as a result of this glorious truth, we are forever adopted into God's family.

> If God is for us, who can be against us? He who did not spare his own Son, but gave him up for us all—how will he not also, along with him, graciously give us all things? Who will bring any charge against those whom God has chosen? It is God who justifies. Who then is the one who condemns? No one. Christ Jesus who died—more than that, who was raised to life—is at the right hand of God and is also interceding for us. Who shall separate us from the love of Christ? Shall trouble or hardship or persecution or famine or nakedness or danger or sword? As it is written:

> > "For your sake we face death all day long;
> > we are considered as sheep to be
> > slaughtered."

> No, in all these things we are more than conquerors through him who loved us. For I am convinced that neither death nor life, neither angels nor demons, neither the present nor the future, nor any powers, neither height nor depth, nor anything else in all creation, will be able to separate us from the love of God that is in Christ Jesus our Lord. (vv. 31–39)

Peace cannot be manufactured—not with pills or programs. Genuine peace comes from only one place: a heart at rest in the Prince of Peace. Friends, when you read the news headlines and it seems as if darkness is winning or when you face your own battles with fear or temptation, remind yourself that Jesus has overcome. When accusations rise against you, plant your feet on the fact that you belong to Him and that nothing can separate you from His love. Let the peace of God rule your heart as you look for hope in His promises.

Think back to the children of Israel at the Red Sea. While Moses looked at his circumstances through eyes of faith, the rest of the people ran to the crazy place of panic. They did not have peace. But we can. When we secure our feet in the gospel of peace, something supernatural occurs: the truth that we are God's beloved children transforms how we experience every circumstance.

The first three pieces of armor—the belt of truth, breastplate of righteousness, and shoes of peace—are those that we put on. With them, we are dressed for victory. They are our daily wardrobe and work in tandem to give our hearts confidence that we are victorious children of God. When we put on this armor, we are defended from the majority of the daily struggles we face. The next chapter will examine the three pieces of armor that we "take up" when under specific attack from the flaming arrows of the Evil One: the shield of faith, helmet of salvation, and sword of the Spirit.

Chapter 8

. . . .

RESIST HIM!

Your enemy the devil prowls around like a roaring lion looking
for someone to devour. Resist him, standing firm in the faith.

1 Peter 5:8–9

No one prepared me for the drastic change that would occur once I got married. I was prepared for a name change, an address change, and a status change. But the one thing I was absolutely unprepared for when I crossed the "I do" threshold was the physical change that happened once my title changed from Miss to Mrs.

I'm talking about the "fat and happy" weight gain that comes with marital bliss.

Perhaps I could blame the domestic diva that took over my body—the one who suddenly felt the need to bake casseroles and cupcakes every day. Or maybe, just maybe, it was the fact that we stayed up late at night our first year of marriage watching *Friday Night Lights* on Netflix while munching cereal. I can't quite blame the nuptials entirely, but I will confess that I was shocked when, after the first year of wedded bliss, I had gained a whole dress size.

One day I finally got fed up with my clothes not fitting, so I decided to do something about it. We cut out our late-night cereal indulgence (RIP Raisin Bran), and I decided to buy a workout video advertised on TV. For those of you who don't know me, here's a little fact: I love infomercials. You know, those thirty-minute commercials filled with amazing before-and-after stories. I am a big fan of any transformation: dirty carpet that looks brand-new, acne-prone skin turned baby soft, or a dramatic weight-loss story. I am not safe around infomercials. I've pretty much purchased everything: skin creams, exercise machines, food storage contain-ers. Buying the latest fitness video was right up my alley.

I'll never forget the day the package arrived. I was full of hope that the extra weight I'd packed on would be gone in just twenty-one days. I opened the DVD, popped it into the player, and hit play. A few minutes in, I realized a big problem: I was sitting on my couch, in my pajamas, eating chips and salsa. Yep, you read that right. Sure, I learned the moves. Sure, I watched other people break a sweat. Sure, I felt motivated. But I didn't do a single thing to *apply* what I was learning. It's not enough to know that something is true; we must put it into action.

I needed to get up, stand on my feet, and actually exercise. I could know all day long that lunges and burpees burn calories, but if I didn't get off my tail and do the burpees, I would never experience transformation.

Faith is not passive; it is active. There is a vast difference between having a knowledge of truth and believing the truth. We can learn Scripture day in and day out, but information alone does nothing to resist the Enemy. The realities we face on a daily basis as believers require us to put feet to our faith and stand.

We might sit in church or attend Bible studies and learn amazing truths about God but remain defeated if we don't learn to resist the Enemy and stand firm in our faith. We can hear testimony after testimony of victory and watch others live out their faith, but all our learning doesn't help if we don't put into action what we know. All too often we sit on our proverbial spiritual couches, eating chips and salsa while other people experience victory.

To stand firm against the Enemy, we have to engage with truth, not just know the truth. We must put into practice the power and privileges we have as children of God. Many Christians can quote Scripture but do not live it. We must do both if we are going to stand firm in victory.

This call to action is essential to utilizing the final three elements in the armor of God. These pieces are ones that must be taken up in the midst of battle and used. It is not enough to know we possess the shield of faith and the sword of the Spirit; we must be people who take up our swords and stand firm behind our shields. Notice the repetition of the commands "put on" and "take" in this passage:

> Stand therefore, having fastened on the belt of truth, and having *put on* the breastplate of righteousness, and, as shoes for your feet, having *put on* the readiness given by the gospel of peace. In

all circumstances *take up* the shield of faith, with
which you can extinguish all the flaming darts
of the evil one; and *take* the helmet of salvation,
and the sword of the Spirit, which is the word of
God. (Eph. 6:14–17 ESV)

As we wrestle against the rulers, authorities, and cosmic powers of this present darkness, we do not sit back and let the Enemy walk all over us. Instead, we take up the full armor of God and we stand. In the previous chapter, we examined the elements of armor that soldiers wear at all times. Now let's turn our attention to the ones that they take up in the midst of battle.

THE SHIELD OF FAITH

Paul warned us that we will be under attack from "flaming arrows of the evil one" (Eph. 6:16). Archeologists inform us that in ancient warfare, armies employed arrows tipped with fire to launch against their opponents. Just imagine you're on a battlefield as fire rains down upon you. The first instinct in such a moment is to duck and cover—to find a place to hide from the onslaught.

Although we don't face physical fiery darts, we do experience them in the spiritual realm. These are strategic and targeted attacks of the Enemy. They especially appeal to our weaknesses, desires, appetites, and lusts, which the opposition hopes will ignite a firestorm of sin in our souls.

These fiery darts could be a sudden onslaught of temptation to sexual sin or an intense struggle with an addiction. Flaming arrows can also mean our jealousy, envy, pride, vanity, insecurities, and greed. These also could be sudden attacks of doubt or an extreme struggle with anger. Or as I described in my battle with rejection, the fiery darts can take the form of mental assaults that hurl themselves against our minds. The bottom line is that the flaming arrows of the Evil One target our flesh (the old sinful nature) and seek to destroy our lives. These mental assaults are more than mere temptation to sin; they are orchestrated attacks designed to take us out.

What about you? What situation in your life feels like a fiery dart targeted at your heart?

Fiery darts target our weaknesses. I know a man who struggles with anger. Although he is a man of great faith, loves God, serves Him faithfully, and believes the Bible, time and time again, flaming arrows of temptation strike and he is enticed to explode. Why this particular temptation? Satan knows that nothing destroys his Christian witness faster, nothing makes him feel more shame, than when he loses his temper. Anger is completely rooted in fear. The Enemy recognizes this man's weak spots and intentionally targets those areas where fear resides. As a little boy, this individual was deeply wounded when life was out of his control; in similar scenarios now, his greatest temptation is to become angry. To resist the Enemy and stand firm, this man has learned to pause and take up his shield of faith. Sometimes this is a silent prayer for the Holy Spirit to help him hold his temper or a verbal proclamation that God is in control. Either way, his victory is found when he actively resists the Enemy by silencing his fears with faith.

I also have a friend walking through a gut-wrenching divorce. She loves Jesus and never in a million years thought this would be her path. Right now she's fighting to stand firm in the midst of the most difficult season of her life. The call to resist the Enemy is a real one, and she feels the fiery darts of temptation descend on a daily basis. His plan in all of this is to tempt her to forsake Jesus. She texted me recently and shared how she is actively resisting the lure to soothe her heartache through false comforts. Whether that is the temptation to sin sexually or drown her pain in alcohol, she now recognizes Satan's agenda. She knows she can't sit back and let the darkness win. I'm so proud of how she is actively choosing to resist him. In moments of weakness, she lifts high the shield of faith and proclaims that Jesus is far better than any of the false comforts Satan wants her to choose. Today she's in a season in which she has to daily take up her shield of faith in order to stand against Satan's schemes.

The shield of faith is perfectly designed to defend us against such assaults. The Roman soldier's shield was much more mighty than just a small piece of metal in front of his body. His shield was more like a door held above his head to protect him from the flaming arrows from above. Historians tell us that the Roman shield was approximately two feet by four feet of wood covered in leather.

What is our shield from the Enemy's attacks? First of all, faith is our supernatural covering. I use the word *supernatural* intentionally, for faith does not operate in the realm of our five senses. Faith works in the unseen realm. The Bible defines faith this way:

"Confidence in what we hope for and assurance about what we do not see" (Heb. 11:1). Just like Moses at the Red Sea, we choose to believe, trust, and obey God even when our physical eyes cannot see the evidence. The flaming arrows of temptation, fear, doubt, condemnation, and accusation will fly at us, intending to set our souls on fire, but we can take up our shield of faith!

TAKE UP YOUR SHIELD OF FAITH!

When flaming arrows of *temptation* fall, the shield of faith believes God's commands are right and for our best. When we trust Him, obey His commands, and choose to walk in His truth, we stop the attack of the Evil One, who seeks to destroy us through sin.

When flaming arrows of *doubt* fall, the shield of faith believes God's Word despite how we feel. Feelings are trumped by faith. Feelings submit to truth. When we raise the shield of faith, we declare truth to our hearts, and our feelings follow suit.

When flaming arrows of *condemnation* fall, the shield of faith covers us by reminding us that we belong to Jesus and there is no condemnation for those in Him.

When flaming arrows of *fear* fall, the shield of faith is God Himself, who covers us under the shadow of His wings. We remember and take comfort in the fact that He is our covering, our protector, and our defender.

Faith holds fast to who God is and what His promises are. Although we can't see Him, we trust Him. When we lift up the shield of faith, we proclaim the greatness of our God to our own hearts and also to the darkness that attacks us.

I'm most likely under attack prior to serving God in a particular work of ministry. I can't always feel the assault coming, and all too often I am besieged before I've thought to lift up my shield. What I've learned over the years is how powerful this shield is when I actually take it up. What does this look like in reality? When I need to take up my shield, I must speak words of faith out loud. They might be specific scriptures or a worship song. But there is one thing I've seen extinguish the fiery darts faster than anything else: the name of Jesus. When I feel that my heart and mind are under attack, I lift up my shield by simply proclaiming His name out loud. Let me testify from personal experience that the Enemy will not stick around when we lift Jesus high. Supernatural power to defeat the Enemy is unleashed when our shield, the name of Jesus, is lifted up.

- Jesus is our defender.
- Jesus is our victory.
- Jesus is our shield against the Evil One.

When we declare His name and proclaim His praise, the darkness flees! This, my friends, is what it means to take up our shield and resist the Enemy.

THE HELMET OF SALVATION

Recently I discovered a show starring a famous chef who helped struggling restaurants undergo massive turnarounds. The businesses featured were failing due to improper management, poor food quality, or lack of organization. Cue the expert to the rescue! The celebrity chef steps onto the scene, discovers the fundamental problems with the operation, and then gives the owner the tools to bring about change.

Once the problems are exposed, the big meltdown occurs. At the mention of change, the owners come unglued. They've been doing the same things the same ways for years upon years. And now, all of a sudden, they are expected to change everything, which is when the host of the show has his real work cut out for him. Before there is ever to be a change materially, there first must be a change mentally.

In one episode, the restaurant owner could not believe her food was not up to par, even though she was losing customers and facing bankruptcy. It took a good deal of reasoning for the chef to prove to her that her mind-set on this subject was flawed. She desperately needed a change of thinking to see things clearly so that she could implement the teachings from her coach.

The same applies to us. When we come to Christ, we've been doing the same things the same ways for years on end. But to stand in victory, we also require a change of mind, which is why we are equipped with a helmet of salvation. With this particular piece of armor, we now see our identities, circumstances, relationships, and choices as God's children rather than as slaves to sin.

> When the set time had fully come, God sent
> his Son, born of a woman, born under the law,
> to redeem those under the law, that we might
> receive adoption to sonship. Because you are

his sons, God sent the Spirit of his Son into our hearts, the Spirit who calls out, "*Abba*, Father." So *you are no longer a slave, but God's child*; and since you are his child, God has made you also an heir. (Gal. 4:4–7)

The Spirit you received does not make you slaves, so that you live in fear again; rather, the Spirit you received brought about your adoption to sonship. And by him we cry, "*Abba*, Father." (Rom. 8:15)

Slavery to sin comes with a mind-set of fear, failure, rejection, and striving. Before Jesus, we all lived as captives to darkness, void of freedom. But now we are redeemed and set free and must begin to think that way. Just as the business owner on the TV show needed to change her thinking to see things correctly and live differently, so do we. We must take up the helmet of salvation in order to think rightly about God, ourselves, and others.

The following chart shows the mind-set difference between those who wear the helmet of salvation and believe they are children of God and the ones who do not, believing instead that they are slaves to sin. Please examine this chart thoroughly. These truths are essential and life-changing. Nothing proves more vital to our ability to stand firm than knowing who we are as children of God.

Slave to Sin Mind-Set		Child of God Mind-Set
Sees God as Master and keeps a distance out of fear of punishment	**Perception of God**	Sees God as *Abba*, the loving heavenly Father, and enjoys a warm and loving relationship with Him
Compares self to others to find value or significance; struggles with insecurity and low self-worth, which manifests in striving, anxiety, and people pleasing	**Self-Image**	Trusts the love and acceptance of Christ, has a heart at peace and rest, and lives out of a secure identity in Christ
Believes access to God's presence is conditional and based upon behavior, feels the need to earn the way into His presence	**View of God's Presence**	Freely abides in Abba's presence, believes Jesus opened the way and gives unlimited access to the Father, experiences God continually
Lives in fear of failure or punishment, obeys God out of duty not delight	**Motivation for Obedience**	Delights in doing God's will and enjoys the blessings of obedience
Critical of others' faults, can't give grace because doesn't receive grace, often competitive with or envious of others	**Relationships with Others**	Gives the grace and love received from the Father to others, seeks unity and celebrates the success of others
Easily hurt or offended when corrected, lashes out or gives the silent treatment, often blames or deflects, can't be deemed wrong or feels rejected	**View of Correction**	Embraces conviction and correction as blessings and longs for truth that brings freedom from sin, responds with repentance and humility

Think back to when I shared my battle with intense feelings of rejection. There wasn't anything I could do to prevent the Enemy from launching those fiery darts at my mind, but I did have a choice as to whether I believed his lies. If I had worn the helmet of salvation in that season, each of those sick suggestions would have been filtered through a "child of God" mind-set and dismissed. Remember, this piece of armor is one that we must take up in the midst of battle. Because I didn't take up the helmet, I was susceptible to lies and experienced the emotional turmoil that resulted, which I like to call going to the crazy place. As soon as I proclaimed my status as a beloved child and took my stand in the acceptance I have in Christ, I experienced peace as my mind was covered by the helmet of my salvation.

PROTECT YOUR MIND!

I've learned that I need to stop when I feel myself spiraling to the crazy place and ask myself some key questions to determine if I am perceiving myself and the situation correctly and if I'm living according to my identity as a child of God. All too often I've found that I need to reject the old "slave to sin" mind-set and align my thinking with God's truth.

Take a minute to scan the chart on the previous page and prayerfully consider which mind-set category you most often find yourself in. Actively reject the lies and proclaim the truth. Choose today to protect your mind with the helmet of salvation and see yourself as the beloved child of God that you truly are.

THE SWORD OF THE SPIRIT

I was a victim of childhood sexual abuse, and the Enemy wreaked havoc on my self-worth. Abuse of any form is done to not only the physical part of who we are but also our innermost beings. One who is abused physically, verbally, emotionally, or sexually carries the hurt long after the memories have faded or been blocked.

Even though my wounding occurred while I was very young (and though it was unknown to my parents), the ripple effects carried on into adulthood. The reason is that our identities are formed by life experiences. My identity was solidified very early: I believed the lie that I was usable and dirty. As a young woman, I thought I was worthy only of being used physically by a man. I wasn't someone to be cherished. My entire identity orbited around male attention and affirmation. Coupled with this belief that I was usable was the lie that I was shameful. I felt dirty and unwanted because of the pain in my soul. The little girl who was victimized didn't know it wasn't her fault or that she wasn't to blame for what was done to her.

I tell you this story because the Enemy loves to access us through our broken places. It is our deepest places of wounding that leave us susceptible to his attacks. Because I believed as a little girl that I was dirty, I grew up into a young woman who didn't think she was worth a man who would cherish her. I didn't think I could resist sexual sin because I perceived myself to be only usable. Therefore, I gravitated toward unhealthy relationships and didn't stand up for myself when treated like trash.

When I fell in love with Jesus and experienced His grace as a young woman, He set my feet on a path of healing. This too is redemption. Jesus not only forgives the sin committed by us but also heals us of the sin done to us. Jesus is the Great Physician. The places in my soul that no human doctor could touch, Jesus did. My healing took place over several years as Jesus purged the toxic pain in my heart with His love. But the primary place transformation occurred was in my mind. Jesus transformed me from the inside out so I could see myself as He saw me: beloved, cherished, clean, whole, and pure.

I share my experience to show why our final piece of armor proves so crucial to victory. The sword of the Spirit is an offensive weapon. As a redeemed woman of God, I had to learn to take up the sword and use it against the forces of darkness desiring to keep me in bondage to sin, shame, and sickness. Even though I had experienced forgiveness and healing from my past, Satan continually attacked until I learned to stand my ground and pick up my sword.

To understand how powerful this piece of armor is, let's take a look at how it functions in the spiritual realm and how Jesus Himself used it against the Enemy. For starters, we must remember that the Bible says, "The tongue has the power of life and death" (Prov. 18:21). Our words are powerful. With them, we either agree with Jesus, who is the voice of truth, or we agree with the Enemy, who is the "father of lies" (John 8:44). Jesus seeks life, and Satan seeks death. With our words, we align with one or the other. God's Word is supernatural, and when we speak it aloud, proclaiming it with our mouths, then we can defeat the schemes and strategies of the Enemy.

When Paul taught about the armor of God in Ephesians 6:13–17, he concluded with our offensive weapon, the sword of the Spirit. That passage is not the only place where God's Word is described as a sword. In the book of Hebrews, we see a more detailed explanation of the Word: "The word of God is *living* and active, sharper than any two-edged sword, *piercing* to the division of soul and of spirit, of joints and of marrow, and discerning the thoughts and intentions of the heart" (4:12 ESV).

First, God's Word is living. These are not just words on a page or ancient stories; His Word is alive with His power and authority. When we take it up and speak it out loud, we express the very utterances of God.

- His Word is His revealed will.
- His Word is His revealed power.
- His Word is His revealed truth.

Second, the Word of God is piercing. It can cut through the chaos and confusion. It reaches the depths of our thoughts and motivations, slicing through the twisted and intertwined places of pain and heartbreak to bring God's truth and freedom.

Nothing scares the Enemy—who operates in lies, intimidation, and speculation—more than a Christ follower who will stand firm in the revealed will of God and declare it boldly.

When God took me through a season of healing, it began with a renewal of my mind. As I read and was taught Scripture by solid Bible teachers and my own personal study, slowly but surely my thoughts began to align with God's truth. Friends, this is an important step in our freedom, but it is not the only one. It is one thing to have our minds renewed (that is, to wear the helmet of salvation or the shoes of peace), but it's a whole different thing to pick up the sword to defeat the Enemy in the moment of need.

What we must recognize in spiritual warfare is this: the Enemy loves to strike when we are at our weakest. It is in these moments that all the Bible study in the world will not equip us to stand firm unless we know how to utilize the sword of the Spirit. Thankfully, Jesus gives us an up-close look at how God's Word defeats the Evil One.

> Jesus, full of the Holy Spirit, returned from the Jordan and was led by the Spirit in the wilderness for forty days, being tempted by the devil. And he ate nothing during those days. And when they were ended, he was hungry. The devil said to him, "If you are the Son of God, command this stone to become bread." And Jesus answered him, "*It is written*, 'Man shall not live by bread alone.'" And the devil took him up and showed him all the kingdoms of the world in a moment of time, and said to him, "To you I will give all this authority and their glory, for it has been delivered to me, and I give it to whom I will. If you, then, will worship me, it will all be yours." And Jesus answered him, "*It is written*,
>
> 'You shall worship the Lord your God,
> and him only shall you serve.'"

And he took him to Jerusalem and set him on the pinnacle of the temple and said to him, "If you are the Son of God, throw yourself down from here, for it is written,

> 'He will command his angels concerning you,
> to guard you,'

and

> 'On their hands they will bear you up,
> lest you strike your foot against a stone.'"

And Jesus answered him, "*It is said*, 'You shall not put the Lord your God to the test.'" And when the devil had ended every temptation, he departed from him until an opportune time. (Luke 4:1–13 ESV)

Jesus's response acts as the ultimate guidebook for spiritual warfare. We require this guidance because the Devil has many ways to trick us into falling into temptation and doubting our identity.

Satan is an opportunist. The Devil cannot read our minds. He is not all-knowing, but he is a shrewd observer of human behavior. He recognizes when we are tired, weak, or vulnerable. In those moments, we are susceptible to attack. When Satan came after Jesus, he waited until after the forty days of fasting were complete. Jesus was hungry. Satan tempted Jesus to meet a legitimate need (food) in an illegitimate way (not trusting His Father to meet His needs).

We must be on guard. If Jesus, the Son of God, could be tempted, then so can we! We are not immune to Satan's lies and deceptions. It is not a sin to be tempted; it is our response to temptation that matters. Just as the Enemy picked the opportune time to tempt Jesus, so he does with us. If you are dealing with a broken heart, be on guard for the temptation to doubt God's love and goodness. If you are working late hours and feeling exhausted, watch out for the siren call of seduction to find comfort and pleasure in substances or pornography. If you are in a fight with your spouse, beware of the lure of another man or woman.

Satan attacks identity. The Father of Lies slithered up to Jesus and said, "If you are the Son of God ..." (v. 3). Notice he used the word *if*. This is a word of doubt. *If* calls into question the veracity of something. Satan questioned if Jesus was actually who He claimed to be: the Son of God.

Why does he do this? For one simple reason: we behave how we believe. Who we perceive ourselves to be in our innermost being is how we live. For example, when I thought of myself as usable and dirty, I lived as though I were usable and dirty. But when Jesus redeemed me and then my mind was renewed by God's Word, I began to see myself as holy, righteous, and cherished. This new identity produced new behavior.

Therefore, it is not by accident that every piece of our spiritual armor points back to our identity in Christ. God knows that we need to be covered with our true identity to protect us from the Evil One.

If Satan can tempt us to believe that we are not beloved children of God, he can sway us to live contrary to this truth.

Jesus speaks the Word. On three different occasions, Satan tempted Jesus. The Son of God's response each time was to say, "It is written ..." or "It is said ..." He didn't debate or engage in conversation. Instead, He declared the authoritative truth of God's Word. Jesus models for us what it means to stand firm and wield the sword of the Spirit.

There is a massive difference between simply knowing Scripture and proclaiming it. In the midst of temptation, Jesus didn't just open the Bible and read what it said. He opened His mouth and spoke what it said. Jesus didn't reason or argue with Satan, and neither should we. We don't engage in emotional dialogue or try to reason with the tempter; we simply and boldly declare the Word.

Satan cannot stand in the face of truth. Because our Enemy operates in lies, he cannot stand when truth is declared. The Word of God is called a sword because it slices through the lies, deceptions, and accusations and boldly declares that which is absolute and unchanging. We must not depend on our feelings or intellect to reason against temptation; we must speak God's Word.

There is supernatural power when we speak the Word of God. Years after I experienced healing from the sexual abuse in my past, I walked through a season of intense temptation. This temptation targeted my identity. Feeling insecure and rejected (opportune time), the Enemy suggested that I would secure love for myself if I were sexually involved with my boyfriend. The battle was intense and real. At first I didn't recognize it as spiritual warfare; I just thought it was the typical struggle a Christian faces when seeking to walk in purity. But after a few weeks of hearing thoughts that suggested sex was no big deal and God didn't care about purity, I realized that the same Father of Lies who targeted Jesus when He was hungry for food was targeting me while I was hungry for love.

In order to stand firm, I had to declare God's truth. For starters, I had to claim my identity in Christ. I began to speak verses out loud that reminded me of how Jesus had redeemed me from my sinful past and how I was now holy and righteous before God. The more my words agreed with God about my status as His child, the less powerful the pull to sin felt. I also began to speak God's truth concerning sex and purity out loud. I found passages throughout the Bible that declare God's desire for sexual purity. I didn't just read these verses; I spoke them. Satan wanted me to believe I was still the same girl I used to be, but when I stood firm on God's truth and picked up the sword, he was defeated.

PICK UP YOUR SWORD!

I'm so grateful for the power of the sword of the Spirit. By picking up the sword and declaring God's truth, I've experienced real victory, and so can you! It is imperative to victory that we know the Word of God. We can't utilize the sword of the Spirit unless it is in our hearts and on our tongues.

Whatever your struggle is today, God's Word speaks to it. Your temptation might be to doubt God's goodness. Dear friend, pick up your sword and declare His praises. Your temptation might be to steal something. Take up your sword and proclaim your heavenly

Father as your provider. Whatever the lie or lure of the Enemy, we have a sure defense against his schemes. The Word of God stands eternal, and the one who is the thief and liar cannot stand against the sword of the Spirit when it is unleashed.

RESIST HIM

Recently, while speaking to a large gathering of Christians, I felt burdened that many sitting before me felt like victims: victims to the Enemy's schemes; to their own addictions, temptations, and weaknesses; and to worldly influences. While I was extolling the abundant life available in Christ, I sensed that many were living in spiritual defeat simply because they didn't believe that victory was even possible. Unbelief hung like a heavy cloud in the room. Doubt filled their eyes.

I completely get it. For many years, I felt the same. I knew there was a great disconnect between the defeat I experienced and the victory I read on the pages of Scripture. It took many years for me to discover the root of the problem, which was that I did not actually believe the truth!

As I surveyed the room, these words of Jesus thundered in my heart: "You will know the truth, and the truth will set you free" (John 8:32). I understood from personal experience that the primary reason Christ followers live in defeat is that we do not know or do not believe the truth. Although many Christians are somewhat familiar with the basics of spiritual warfare, most don't realize that defeat is not the expectation. The apostle Peter, a man who knew a thing or two about the Enemy's schemes, shared this important word with us:

"Be alert and of sober mind. Your enemy the devil prowls around like a roaring lion looking for someone to devour. *Resist him, standing firm in the faith*" (1 Pet. 5:8–9).

The word *resist* means "to stand one's ground." The Greek root word for *resist* means "to stand firm." It is a military term for firmly holding a position that is under attack. Learning to stand firm in the days of evil begins with recognizing our responsibility to do so. Not only are we to expect opposition but we are also told to stand our ground and resist it.

Friends, we do have a choice in the matter. Yes, we are involved in a cosmic conflict between the kingdom of darkness and the kingdom of God, but the greater reality is this: we are not struggling to win ground; we are called to stand firm in the victory that Jesus Christ already won. We fight *from* a place of victory, not *for* victory.

The Enemy is crushed under the feet of Jesus. This truth, when understood and applied, will absolutely transform how we live. Instead of facing the winds and waves that seek to knock us down with a mind-set of defeat and victimization, we can now respond to them from a place of authority and victory in Christ.

I have a friend who was once tormented by nightmares and spiritual attacks during the night. He woke with a deep feeling of dread and felt a presence in the room. For many weeks, this attack kept him in angst and suffering from exhaustion. He lived in fear and assumed that the spiritual forces coming against him were too powerful to resist.

One day he shared with me and my husband his struggle, and we began to pray and point him to God's Word. We showed him how the Bible tells us that we can indeed resist the Enemy. We looked at passages that give us authority to rebuke him in Jesus's name.

After we exposed Satan's mode of operation, my friend returned home armed with God's truth. The next time we saw him, he was full of peace, joy, and rest. Indeed, the truth had set him free! Instead of spending sleepless nights in fear of the Enemy, he resisted by standing firm in the victory of Christ and taking up the full armor of God.

GREATER IS HE

In the gospel of Matthew, we find the greatest teaching about the kingdom of God and Christ's authority. Jesus, the long-awaited Messiah King, ushers in the kingdom of God, and the darkness reacts in powerful ways: demonic outbursts, blinding hatred, and jealous fury. Throughout this gospel, we see two kingdoms clearly juxtaposed: darkness versus light in a showdown for the souls of humanity and the dominion of earth.

Throughout Matthew, the demonic realm is threatened and lashes out as the Son of God marches toward victory. Jesus's miracles are on display in each gospel, but in Matthew they play a special role: revealing in signs and wonders what His authority looks like on earth. The sick are healed. The blind see. The lame walk. The mute talk. His authority and power over the forces of darkness set captives free and bring life, hope, and healing.

No miracle portrayed His dominion more clearly than when Jesus walked on water. When Jesus walked across the waves in the middle of the night to rescue His weary followers from a storm, it was more than just a Vegas-worthy show of epic proportions. It was a display of authority over the winds and the waves. There is one King, one Lord, one Creator—and Jesus, water-walking Jesus, is His name. All things are under His feet!

With each miracle and every display of power, the disciples watched in wonder at the authority of the King of Kings and Lord of Lords. They marveled as He cast out demons, and they stood shaking in fear as He commanded the winds and waves to be still. Jesus portrayed in living color what it looks like to take authority over the darkness and stand against it.

Then one day it was their turn: "Jesus called his twelve disciples to him and gave them authority to drive out impure spirits and to heal every disease and sickness" (Matt. 10:1). Jesus sent out His disciples into the world as light in the darkness, endowed with power and authority in His name. In doing so, they confronted the kingdom of darkness and rejoiced that the demons submitted to them in His name. What we must understand is that this authority did not end with the last pages of the Bible. Today we also stand firm, resist the Enemy, walk in victory—all in the name of Jesus. We don't have to fall for Satan's schemes, believe his lies, or be intimidated by his threats. As 1 John 4:4 says, "The one who is in you is greater than the one who is in the world."

Comprehending these truths transformed my experience of the Christian life, and I believe it will do the same for you. As we begin to realize we are positioned for victory and can stand against the Enemy in the name of Jesus, our whole perspective shifts when confronted with his schemes. We are not powerless but powerful! We are not victims but victors!

Thanks be to God! He gives us the victory through our Lord Jesus Christ.

Therefore, my dear brothers and sisters, stand firm. Let nothing move you. Always give yourselves fully to the work of the Lord, because you know that your labor in the Lord is not in vain. (1 Cor. 15:57–58)

STAND

· · · · · · · · · · ·

THE PROMISE TO OVERCOMERS

The one who stands firm to the end will be saved.

Matthew 24:13

Chapter 9

· · · · · · ·

STAND WHEN THE WORLD HATES YOU

[Jesus said,] "You will be hated by everyone because of me,
but the one who stands firm to the end will be saved."
Matthew 10:22

Few of us will ever forget the moment we witnessed the brutal execution of the three brave Assyrian men who were shot because of their faith in Christ. Wearing orange jumpsuits and kneeling on the ground, the final moment of their lives was captured for the world to see by terrorists who used the execution to strike fear in others.

As the lifeless bodies of those three men lay in the sand, masked terrorists armed with pistols stood behind three other kneeling Assyrian men. The hostage in the middle, pointing at the bloodied bodies, declared, "Our fate is the same as these if you do not take proper procedure for our release." Before stating their names, the hostages each said, "I am Nasrani," a derogatory Muslim term for Christians.[1]

Our Assyrian brothers died for one reason: the name of Jesus.

"According to the Pew Research Center, 74 percent of the world's population live in a country where social hostilities involving religion are high, and 64 percent live where government restrictions on religion are high."[2] Although this might not be your present situation, the reality is this: persecution is the norm across the globe and is coming rapidly to the West. As Christians, we will face persecution or be hated for our faith.

Jesus prepared us for this experience. After all, He said, "If the world hates you, keep in mind that it hated me first" (John 15:18). Hated because of Jesus? Did the one named Prince of Peace really say this? How can this be true? Surely, the God of all grace, the One who heals the brokenhearted and frees the captive, doesn't expect us to be unpopular, much less hated? How could anyone despise such beautiful gifts as love, grace, and peace? This is one of those Jesus statements that makes me scratch my head, cock it sideways, and ask, "For real?"

It simply defies logic.

Why would the people of grace be reviled? You would think the gospel, the greatest news of all time, would make us the most beloved people in the world. It's kind of crazy to think that the Savior of the world and His followers would be scorned by those He came to save.

But, yep, Jesus sure did say it, and not just once. Every gospel account records Him warning us to expect persecution, contempt, and ridicule. He also gives a promise to the one who stands firm in the midst of it: "Everyone will hate you because of me, but the one who stands firm to the end will be saved" (Mark 13:13).

Those verses in John and Mark are not ones I've highlighted in my Bible with little hearts around them. I also don't see them on social media as anyone's 140-character Twitter post. They are not the ones we display on T-shirts or pretty little wall prints. Please let me know if you see any on a bumper sticker or in the end zone of a football game.

We tend to gravitate toward the fun promises that deal with victory, prosperity, and mercy, but Jesus felt it was essential to prepare us for the reality we would face after His resurrection. The reality is this: if we are truly His disciples, then in the same way the world despised and rejected Him, they will also despise and reject us.

Most of us have never experienced persecution like our brothers and sisters in Christ who live in countries where it is illegal to profess Christianity. For most of us in the West, persecution is something we hear about in church or read about; it has yet to land on our doorsteps. However, I believe that day is coming—and coming soon—when we will share their sufferings. Therefore, if we are to stand firm, we must be prepared to experience backlash and be hated for the name of Christ. After all, the Word of God is clear: "Everyone who wants to live a godly life in Christ Jesus will be persecuted" (2 Tim. 3:12).

Jesus didn't prepare us for a popularity contest. Instead, He lovingly primed us for a world that would misunderstand, mistreat, and malign us. Honestly, the people pleaser in me wants to make this more digestible, but as hard as I try to find a synonym for *hate* that sounds less angry, I can't do it. There is no sugarcoating this verse. It's about as straightforward as you can get.

I don't know about you, but I'm someone who likes to be liked. As early as I can remember, I envisioned myself wanting to fit in and be part of the inner circle. This is human nature. No one I know relishes rejection or exclusion. I want people to think well of me. I want my good intentions to be recognized as such. I want my name to be honored, not ridiculed. I want to be in the cool club. Not many of us sign up for following Jesus hoping that we will be despised because of it, but that is the reality.

Jesus never lied to us. He cautioned that we are in the midst of a world that will oppose our beliefs and persecute us without cause. In this chapter, we will uncover the why behind persecution, but first we must note that the backlash did not take Jesus by surprise. He dedicated the majority of His final hours before His death to preparing the disciples for persecution. The gospel of John gives us an incredible play-by-play of these events.

On the eve of His crucifixion, Jesus celebrated the Feast of Passover with the disciples in Jerusalem. This feast commemorated Israel's redemption from slavery in Egypt and reminded God's people how the covering of the lamb's blood was the key to life and freedom.

As the disciples gathered in the upper room to share the Passover meal, Jesus explained how His broken body and poured-out blood were the final sacrifice to pay for the sins of the world. Throughout Jesus's three years of ministry, He prepared them for His death. At this point, He utilized the visual illustration of the Passover to explain why it must occur. All of redemption history climaxed in His sacrifice. Jesus knew He was the fulfillment of this sacrificial symbol: "The Lamb of God, who takes away the sin of the world!" (John 1:29).

As the Passover meal concluded, the Lamb of God left the symbolic meal to face His destiny. He led the disheartened group to the garden of Gethsemane, where Jesus knew His betrayer, Judas, would find Him with the Roman guards and Jewish leaders. En route to the garden, He paused for a few final teachable moments with the men who would carry His message of grace and freedom to the world.

These teachable moments form the framework for life in Christ. Jesus's words from two thousand years ago equip us to stand firm today against a world that reviles us. Therefore, let's slip into the cool Jerusalem night and stand with the disciples as they hear the Master impart wisdom concerning the days ahead.

TO STAND WHEN PERSECUTED, WE MUST ABIDE

Jesus, the Son of God, knew all the things that were soon to happen to Him: His betrayal, arrest, beatings, rejection, and horrific death by crucifixion. Yet in the midst of His greatest moment of suffering, He loved His own enough to prepare them for the dark days they would face.

Walking by torchlight, the disciples trekked up the Kidron Valley toward the garden. First, Jesus stopped at a vineyard. Pausing, He imparted the key to living the Christian life. He picked up a common grape vine and illustrated how life for a disciple is one of complete reliance. Just as a branch is completely dependent on the vine for life and will die if separated from it, we rely on Jesus. Apart from Him, we can do nothing! Always the master teacher, Jesus takes the ordinary and teaches the extraordinary. Nothing could be more simple, yet at the same time, no truth proves more profound. We are made one with Christ, and in this union, His Spirit fills and flows through us, producing His righteous character.

> *Abide* in me, and I in you. As the branch cannot bear fruit by itself, unless it *abides* in the vine, neither can you, unless you *abide* in me. I am the vine; you are the branches. Whoever *abides* in me and I in him, he it is that bears much fruit, for apart from me you can do nothing. (John 15:4–5 ESV)

Notice the relational language Jesus used to describe this spiritual union. Multiple times we are called to abide. This term means to "take up residence" in Jesus and make our home in Him. We are intrinsically connected to Him, and through this abiding relationship, His life is manifested in us. As a result of this supernatural connection, three things occur:

- The spiritual fruit that is produced glorifies the Father and proves we are His disciples.
- This abiding relationship is the source of our ultimate joy.
- The evidence of Jesus's life within us causes the world to hate us.

I try to imagine how John heard this call to abide. For three unforgettable years, he walked and talked with Jesus. Day in and day out, His physical presence was all John knew. He beheld His glory. He witnessed His miracles. He marveled at His mercy.

Could John, the Beloved Disciple, even comprehend life apart from Jesus? Everything Jesus shared with His disciples in those few short hours was to prepare them for the years ahead when His physical presence would not be with them.

Keep in mind, every word of this conversation was meant to equip the disciples for life after the resurrection. Jesus plainly stated that He was going to the Father and would no longer be with them. Yet strangely, at the same time, His call was clear: "Abide in me." Thankfully, He didn't leave this new relationship a mystical mystery. Jesus explained the new relationship would be one by and through the Holy Spirit.

> All this I have spoken while still with you. But the Advocate, the Holy Spirit, whom the Father will send in my name, will teach you all things and will remind you of everything I have said to you. Peace I leave with you; my peace I give you. I do not give to you as the world gives. Do not let your hearts be troubled and do not be afraid. (John 14:25–27)

Those who abide in Christ, indwelled by the Spirit, are the ones who will carry His name to the world. We are His ambassadors, endowed with supernatural power and authority to be light in the darkness. Ironically, it is this very light that the darkness despises. It is the presence of Christ in the world, displayed through His church, that evokes the hatred and rage of the kingdom of darkness.

So far, Jesus's words were meant to encourage the struggling crew to hope. He knew that the disciples were weighed down by sadness at the prospect of His death. His promise of an enduring, abiding relationship was meant to bring peace and hope in the midst of that dark night. But just as soon as He comforted them with those promises, He prepared them for pending persecution.

Essentially, the reason we must abide in Him and the reason we require the dynamic power of the Holy Spirit is that we are sent out into the world as "sheep among wolves" (Matt. 10:16).

> If the world hates you, keep in mind that it hated me first. If you belonged to the world, it would love you as its own. As it is, you do not belong to the world, but I have chosen you out of the world. That is why the world hates you. Remember what I told you: "A servant is not greater than his master." If they persecuted me, they will persecute you also. If they obeyed my teaching, they will obey yours also. They will treat you this way because of my name, for they do not know the one who sent me. (John 15:18–21)

Friends, Jesus cautioned us because He wanted us to stand firm. Can you imagine how shocked and disillusioned the early disciples would have been if Jesus had not warned them of the fate that awaited them? The early church endured horrific persecution for the name of Christ. A hefty percentage of the early followers of Christ died martyrs' deaths. Peter was crucified, Paul beheaded, and Stephen stoned to death. Even though John didn't face a martyr's death, it wasn't because Rome didn't try. Historians tell us that he was boiled alive for his faith in Christ and for refusing to worship the emperor. John was saved supernaturally, but not all were so fortunate.

What if the disciples had been blindsided by the world's hatred? Can you imagine how hard it would have been to stand firm if they'd felt tricked or misguided by their Master? For this reason, Jesus shot straight with them:

> *All this I have told you so that you will not fall away.* They will put you out of the synagogue; in fact, the time is coming when anyone who kills you will think they are offering a service to God. They will do such things because they have not known the Father or me. *I have told you this, so that when their time comes you will remember that I warned you about them.* I did not tell you this from the beginning because I was with you. (John 16:1–4)

Notice that He told them these things so that they would not "fall away." Falling away is the exact opposite of standing firm. To fall away means to lose faith, to forsake the call, and to forfeit the crown of life. Jesus knows that the Enemy unleashes persecution on us for this very reason, so He prepares us to stand.

HATERS GONNA HATE

Perhaps you're reading this and asking, "Can't we all just get along?" Why can't we show mercy and win over the haters? Surely, if we exhibit

Christ's love, the world will see Him and embrace us, right? The answer is complicated. Yes, our love is a powerful witness to the lost world, but Jesus also promised that we would be hated on account of His name.

Why all the hate?

There are two reasons. The first is that there are two opposing kingdoms at war. The kingdom of darkness, otherwise known as "the world," is ruled by Satan, and it seeks to usurp the one true God. The kingdom of God is ruled by Jesus, who defeated Satan at the cross and in doing so rescued captives from his domain. Note how the following verses explain these two kingdoms at war:

> [God] has *rescued us from the kingdom of darkness* and transferred us into the Kingdom of his dear Son. (Col. 1:13 NLT)

> Do not love the world or anything in the world. *If anyone loves the world, love for the Father is not in them.* For everything in the world—the lust of the flesh, the lust of the eyes, and the pride of life—comes not from the Father but from the world. (1 John 2:15–16)

> We know that we are children of God, and that *the whole world is under the control of the evil one.* (1 John 5:19)

These verses paint a very clear reality: all human beings follow one of two kingdoms. There is no neutral ground. There is no Switzerland in this war.

Throughout history, darkness has sought to destroy Jesus and His own. For example, when Jesus was just a baby, King Herod ordered every child under the age of two to be murdered. Then, during Jesus's ministry, the religious leaders, fueled with their own demonic jealousy, plotted to kill Him. Without cause, the leaders instigated His crucifixion. These are just two examples in the life of Christ of how the kingdom of darkness tried to destroy the kingdom of light.

When ministering in India a few years ago, I met a young pastor who had experienced this same unwarranted hatred firsthand. His effervescent joy in Christ made me forget his horrific background and the painful experiences that led him to flee his home village. When I met this young man, he was enrolled in a pastoral training school. He stood out among all the students. His smile was radiant, his worship unbridled. When he spoke of Jesus, his eyes brimmed with tears. I could never have imagined that a man so consumed with love for the Lord would have endured such intense persecution.

As a teenager, he heard the gospel from missionaries visiting his small village. The missionary team gave him a copy of the New Testament, and he took it home, reading it in secret each night. His faith in Jesus grew and soon became evident to his family. Even though he had been threatened with expulsion, he didn't deny his faith in Christ. Eventually, the leaders of his village severely beat him, tossed him into a barrel, and rolled him out of town. Although he was rejected by family and friends and physically tortured, his passion for Jesus could not be contained. The darkness raged against him, but it did not overcome the light. What amazed me about this young man's story is this: he was studying theology to become a pastor so that he could return to his home village to plant a church! As Jesus said, "The gates of hell shall not prevail against [the church]" (Matt. 16:18 ESV).

The second reason the world hates Jesus and His followers is that light exposes darkness. Just think about it: Those who practice evil prefer the cover of night. In the same way, those who are still enslaved to Satan and in bondage to sin prefer to remain in the dark. They resent and hate the light that exposes sinful deeds. In the gospel of John, Jesus described the problem this way:

> Light has come into the world, but people loved darkness instead of light because their deeds were evil. Everyone who does evil hates the light, and will not come into the light for fear that their deeds will be exposed. But whoever lives by the truth comes into the light, so that it may be seen plainly that what they have done has been done in the sight of God. (John 3:19–21)

Jesus is the Light of the World. When He enters a room, the radiance of His glory exposes what is unrighteous and dark. The one who hates a Christian is often unaware of why he is reacting in such a hostile way; he isn't cognizant that the sin within him desires to remain hidden and is threatened by the presence of Jesus. Because the Spirit of God lives in us, we carry His presence into the world. That is why Jesus said,

You are the light of the world. A town built on a hill cannot be hidden. Neither do people light a lamp and put it under a bowl. Instead they put it on its stand, and it gives light to everyone in the house. In the same way, let your light shine before others, that they may see your good deeds and glorify your Father in heaven. (Matt. 5:14–16)

As the Light of the World, we glorify God with His Son's radiance in us. Our actions should reflect the Lord's righteousness and holiness. Throughout the history of the church, it was this light that won over many from the kingdom of darkness, but at the same time, it was this light that evoked anger in those who hated it.

A close friend of mine works in a secular environment that is hostile to Christian values. While preaching tolerance, they prove intolerant of anyone who holds to biblical beliefs. Christ followers there are labeled bigots and ridiculed as ignorant. There seems little my friend can say or do to contradict the fixed stigma. Although she exhibits Christ's character and is known for humility, honesty, generosity, and kindness, she is often excluded and alienated in the workplace. It's as if her very presence evokes anger in some. The light of Christ within her exposes the emptiness and darkness around her. Unredeemed human nature is hostile toward God. As a result, some of the coworkers react harshly without even knowing why they are doing so. The presence of Christ, in any environment, causes a reaction.

Part of the world's hatred is fueled by a demonic obsession with opposing Jesus and His church. This, my friends, is just another brand of spiritual warfare. Another reason for the animosity is the conviction experienced by the world when the presence of Jesus is felt. Today Jesus is made known to the world through the church, so the church lives as light in the darkness, and the darkness reacts, often harshly.

GO AND STAND!

I love God's Word. Not only has Scripture transformed my life and healed my soul, but in seasons of testing, it empowers me to stand. Although I've never faced the intense physical persecution that my brothers and sisters across the globe endure, I can share my own tales of ridicule, intimidation, and hostility for my belief in Jesus and proclamation of the gospel.

As an evangelist, I've shared my faith on more than 150 college campuses. Let me just say, these secular settings are not always the friendliest of venues. Not only is there a palpable apathy toward God, but there is also a high sense of political correctness that bristles at absolute truth and our need for salvation from sin. The gospel we preach opposes the world's philosophies, and, as stated earlier, the darkness hates the light. Therefore, I've been called to stand firm often as people vocalize their anger at the message and blatantly walk out of the room whenever the name of Jesus is mentioned.

On too many occasions, I quaked with the fear of man, being intimidated by those who reject me for my beliefs and questioning my message when spurned. These moments make me forever grateful for the saints of God who stood firm for the truth in the midst of hostile environments by holding their ground and declaring Jesus as the only hope for humanity.

One such story is that of Peter and John. The setting of this hostile attack on faith is shortly after Jesus's ascension to heaven (see Acts 1:9–11). Jesus's bodily resurrection from the grave so changed these men that they would go from fearfully denying Him to boldly proclaiming that He is Lord and God.

As a result of Peter and John's unflinching faith, the same religious leaders who conspired to kill Jesus were fed up with the little band of zealots. To make matters worse, not only were the disciples preaching Jesus, but in His name they also performed miracles. They were empowered by the Spirit of God, just as Jesus promised they would be. The glorious light radiating from the apostles led thousands from darkness to the living God.

We pick up their story at an incredible intersection. Arrested for sharing the good news and thrown in jail as a result, the apostles were miraculously set free by an angel of the Lord in the middle of the night. Instead of taking their get-out-of-jail-free card and running for safety, they obeyed the angel's command to "go, stand ... and tell the people all about this new life" (Acts 5:20). Their call was not to hide from the opposition but to take the light into the very den of darkness and let it shine. Their obedience teaches us how to respond to persecution.

> The high priest and all his associates, who were members of the party of the Sadducees, were filled with jealousy. They arrested the apostles and put them in the public jail. But during the night an angel of the Lord opened the doors of the jail and brought them out. "Go, stand in the temple courts," he said, "and tell the people all about this new life."

At daybreak they entered the temple courts, as they had been told, and began to teach the people. (Acts 5:17–21)

The disciples obeyed the angel and returned to the streets of Jerusalem, declaring the life found only in Jesus. The dramatic account of their release and their refusal to remain silent made its way back to the ears of the religious leaders. Once again, the disciples were called to stand trial for their faith.

The apostles were brought in and made to appear before the Sanhedrin to be questioned by the high priest. "We gave you strict orders not to teach in this name," he said. "Yet you have filled Jerusalem with your teaching and are determined to make us guilty of this man's blood."

Peter and the other apostles replied: "*We must obey God rather than human beings!* The God of our ancestors raised Jesus from the dead—whom you killed by hanging him on a cross. God exalted him to his own right hand as Prince and Savior that he might bring Israel to repentance and forgive their sins. We are witnesses of these things, and so is the Holy Spirit, whom God has given to those who obey him." (vv. 27–32)

Standing firm in their faith, the apostles boldly declared the truth and did not waver even when threatened. As a result, they were *flogged*.

Don't speed past that word and lose the impact of their suffering. For the name of Jesus, they were beaten with whips until they bled. After the flogging, Scripture concludes,

> [The Sanhedrin] ordered them not to speak in the name of Jesus, and let them go.
>
> *The apostles left the Sanhedrin, rejoicing because they had been counted worthy of suffering disgrace for the Name.* Day after day, in the temple courts and from house to house, they never stopped teaching and proclaiming the good news that Jesus is the Messiah. (vv. 40–42)

The apostles stood firm in their faith, proclaiming the new life available to all who believe in Jesus. Their motivation was love for others and desire for them to experience salvation and obedience to the call of God on their lives. Fulfilling Jesus's call to be the "light of the world" (Matt. 5:14), they didn't hide; instead, they let Christ shine brightly, no matter the cost. Peter rightly responded to the men seeking to destroy him, "We must obey God rather than human beings!" (Acts 5:29).

I firmly believe we are approaching a day in which each of us must make that same decision. Our choice to believe, obey, and live for Jesus will not be popular; in fact, it will be hated. We must make the decision in advance to stand. We must make the decision in advance to obey God rather than human beings. The Holy Spirit of God will enable and empower us to stand firm as we encounter these circumstances. Whether we are called names or called to stand trial, the Lord will not leave or abandon us. Jesus is with us! The same Spirit who raised Jesus from the dead dwells with us. He will give you and me the words to speak, the courage to hold our ground, the wisdom to respond, and the power to forgive. Whenever persecution comes, and it will, our ability to stand firm will come from the very same power source that fueled Peter and John before the Sanhedrin: the Spirit of the living God.

Perhaps the most startling aspect of this story is the apostles' response to the flogging and punishment. I hope you didn't miss it, because Scripture tells us that they rejoiced! They celebrated because they saw their circumstances from an eternal perspective instead of a temporal one. They rejoiced because they could see that their stand for Christ threatened the kingdom of darkness; if it didn't, the kingdom of darkness wouldn't react so violently. These men also knew that the gates of hell cannot prevail against the church and that, at the end of the day, Jesus wins. These facts filled their hearts with joy, and it should fill ours too!

Perhaps you can't relate to the anger and hostility that is the norm for most Christ followers across the globe. If that's the case, we will discover what you can do in the meantime. But for those of you who are feeling the heat and bearing the brunt of others' animosity, I want to encourage you and remind you of our biblical response to the world's hatred. Jesus is clear. We have two responses to persecution: rejoice when it happens, and bless those who do it.

REJOICE!

Just as the apostles rejoiced when imprisoned and flogged for the name of Jesus, we should count it a privilege that we are included in their ranks. Jesus not only prepared us for this reality but He also promised that we would be greatly rewarded in heaven if we stood strong.

> Blessed are you when people insult you, persecute you and falsely say all kinds of evil against you because of me. *Rejoice* and be glad, because great is your reward in heaven, for in the same way they persecuted the prophets who were before you. (Matt. 5:11–12)

Our response as Christ followers is to fix our eyes on Jesus and our hope in heaven. In the next and final chapter, we will carefully unpack the eternal rewards awaiting those who overcome. Keep in mind, persecution purifies our hearts and increases our longing for our true heavenly home. No wonder the apostle Peter wrote so much about it in his letters. Not only was he suffering alongside others in the early church but he also knew he must encourage others not to lose hope.

> Dear friends, do not be surprised at the fiery ordeal that has come on you to test you, as though something strange were happening to you. But *rejoice* inasmuch as you participate in the sufferings of Christ, so that you may be overjoyed when his glory is revealed. If you are insulted because of the name of Christ, you are blessed, for the Spirit of glory and of God rests on you. If you suffer, it should not be as a murderer or thief or any other kind of criminal,

or even as a meddler. However, if you suffer as a
Christian, do not be ashamed, but praise God that
you bear that name. (1 Pet. 4:12–16)

Just as Moses's call to Israel at the Red Sea to stand and see was
counterintuitive (see Exod. 14:13–14), so it seems that the call to
rejoice when persecuted proves illogical. Why would one celebrate
when insulted? Peter gave us the answer when he said, "The Spirit of
glory and of God rests on you" (1 Pet. 4:14). As redeemed sons and
daughters of God, we should celebrate that the world can see Christ
in us. We aren't hated because of who we are; we are hated because
of who Jesus is. The presence of Jesus is a mirror, and those enslaved
to the Enemy don't want to look in that mirror and see their sin and
darkness; therefore, they react harshly.

If you thought the first response seemed contradictory, just wait
until you hear the second one. The Bible repeatedly calls us to follow
in Jesus's example and bless those who persecute us.

BLESS

I don't know about you, but I'm a fighter. I'm not talking MMA
(mixed martial arts), nor do I like physical violence. But when
pushed down, something rises up in me and I want to push back.
When treated wrongly, my first instinct isn't "kill 'em with kindness."
When I'm cut off by rude drivers in traffic, I won't lie and say my
reflex is always a good one. That is my flesh, otherwise known as
the old sinful nature. Our flesh is selfish; it wants to be right, and it
wants to retaliate when wronged. Therefore, when I read the biblical

commands to bless those who persecute, insult, or harm us, I realize first and foremost that this is a supernatural response. This is not a flesh response. God calls us to do something that is possible *only* by the power of His Holy Spirit.

> Bless those who persecute you; bless and do not curse. (Rom. 12:14)

> Do not repay evil with evil or insult with insult. On the contrary, repay evil with blessing, because to this you were called so that you may inherit a blessing. (1 Pet. 3:9)

> If your enemy is hungry, give him food to eat;
>   if he is thirsty, give him water to drink.
>   (Prov. 25:21)

Why does the Lord want such a radical response? I believe this supernatural, Spirit-led reaction to persecution glorifies God because it testifies to the radical transformation that occurs in the human heart when Jesus is on the throne. Sure, it is human nature to retaliate, but it is Jesus's nature to bless. Just think back to the very first family and the original hatred in it. Adam and Eve had two sons: Cain and Abel. Shortly after sin entered the world came the bitter fruit of hatred. Cain killed his brother Abel. That is how the flesh responds to a relational conflict. Although we might not kill with our hands as Cain did, all too often we hurt others with our words or hold on to angry bitterness toward them in our hearts.

Jesus's response, on the other hand, was the exact opposite. While He was on the cross, dying for the sins of the world, hate-filled Jewish leaders and Roman soldiers circled like a swarm of predators, hurling insults. His response to His persecutors was this: "Father, forgive them, for they do not know what they are doing" (Luke 23:34). He could have easily called a legion of angels to His defense or opened the ground beneath the mockers' feet to consume them whole, but He didn't. He modeled undeserved mercy. He knew His battle was not against "flesh and blood" (Eph. 6:12) but against a spiritual Enemy who influenced and fueled His persecutors' hatred. He could forgive those who hurt Him by recognizing that they were merely pawns in the hands of the real Enemy. Satan is the true mastermind behind persecution.

Friends, Jesus lives within us. When we forsake our fleshly desire for retaliation and allow the Holy Spirit to pour into our hearts His love, grace, and forgiveness, we can radically obey God when He says to bless those who persecute us. And guess what? He promises us that those who obey will be greatly rewarded in heaven! We'll see more on that topic in the next chapter.

And really, what other option do we have than to bless? If we don't bless, we will be consumed with the same hatred and bitterness that fill the ones hurting us. I believe that God calls us to bless others in order to protect us from the poison of unforgiveness and shine Jesus into the darkest of environments, which is our ultimate calling after all.

The world takes notice when our reactions are different. Think about the impact and legacy of Martin Luther King Jr. In an age of bigotry and hatred, King responded with forgiveness, peace, and grace. By obeying the commands of God to turn the other cheek and bless his enemies, King was able to bring about the greatest changes in civil rights issues in the United States. When we love, bless, pray, provide, and care for the ones who would hurt us, this Spirit-filled response testifies to God's transforming grace and changes hearts.

Church history is replete with stories of how faithful Christian martyrs influenced the world. While facing the gladiators of Rome or other horrific deaths, men and women of the early church stood firm in the faith and often prayed for and blessed the ones harming them. Because of the saints' faithfulness, the Roman Empire ultimately turned from darkness to light in a short three hundred years. The believers' firm stance in their faith, Spirit-filled response, and love for their enemies preached a sermon that turned an empire upside down and spread the church across the globe. History proves that God's ways work. Our flesh might scream a message of retaliation, but the Spirit of God calls us to bless, and when we do so, our obedience could mean another's salvation.

Perhaps you are like me and you find yourself feeling very far removed from the atrocities across the world that other Christians face. God's Word says that when one part of the body suffers, we all suffer (see 1 Cor. 12:26). Therefore, our role is to stand with and pray for those who are presently enduring the wrath of the Enemy. The Bible calls us to be a voice for the voiceless. Psalm 82:3 says, "Defend the weak and the fatherless; uphold the cause of the poor and the oppressed." And Hebrews 13:3 says, "Continue to remember those in prison as if you were together with them in prison, and those who are mistreated as if you yourselves were suffering." The following ministries are incredible organizations that aid persecuted Christians around the world and offer tools to help us know how to pray for them: the Voice of the Martyrs (www.persecution.com) and Open Doors (www.opendoorsusa.org).

Chapter 10

. . . .

WIN LIFE!

I heard a loud voice in heaven say: "Now have
come the salvation and the power and the
kingdom of our God, and the authority of his
Messiah. For the accuser of our brothers and
sisters, who accuses them before our God day and
night, has been hurled down. They triumphed
over him by the blood of the Lamb and by
the word of their testimony; they did not love
their lives so much as to shrink from death.

Revelation 12:10–11

Wilma Rudolph was the epitome of an overcomer. The twentieth of
twenty-two children, she was a premature baby who weighed only
four and a half pounds. Her mother feared she wouldn't survive to
her first birthday, yet survive she did!

Wilma lived through her infancy, only to face more obstacles. At the age of four, she contracted double pneumonia, and scarlet fever, leaving her left leg paralyzed. Her mother was determined to take her once a week to receive special treatment. At the age of six, Wilma started to hop on one leg. And miraculously, she began walking with a leg brace at eight years old. Still pressing on and never giving up, she continued to fight against her infirmity, determined not to be a victim to it. Through sheer resolve, an orthopedic shoe eventually replaced her leg brace. Then one day, when she was only eleven years old, she could finally play basketball barefoot. That day marked the end of the paralyzed, sick, little girl and the beginning of a legendary sports hero.

Wilma began her love of sports as a basketball player, but her passion for running would determine her destiny. In 1956, at the young age of sixteen, she ran in the Melbourne Olympics, taking home a bronze medal in the four-hundred-meter relay. Just think about it: she'd only been walking without the assistance of a brace for five years and was already an Olympic medalist!

Then, after graduating high school, she attended Tennessee State University and went on to compete in the 1960 Olympics. The day before the hundred meters, she stepped into a hole and twisted an ankle. Resolved to run, she wouldn't quit. The next day, she won her semifinal in 11.3 seconds despite her injury. She was the first American woman to win three gold medals in track and field at a single Olympics.

When "The Star-Spangled Banner" played and Wilma Rudolph took her stand on the podium, she modeled the champion spirit of one who overcomes seemingly insurmountable obstacles to stand victorious.[1]

OVERCOMERS

I love a good account of an overcomer. Comeback stories strike a chord in us because we see something of ourselves in the script. Life is difficult. We endure challenges, setbacks, and an Enemy who seeks to take us out. Over the past nine chapters, we've examined the real-life situations that topple our faith and leave us defeated. Yet we follow the One who is the ultimate overcomer! Jesus overcame Satan, conquered sin, and defeated death to rise again and stand victorious for us. Jesus calls us to follow Him and stand firm in the victory He accomplished: "I have told you these things, so that in me you may have peace. In this world you will have trouble. But take heart! I have overcome the world" (John 16:33).

We started this journey with Jesus's promise "Stand firm, and you will win life" (Luke 21:19). Throughout the book of Revelation, Jesus praised the ones who stand firm against darkness, temptation, and persecution. The word He used repeatedly to describe those victorious saints was *overcomer*: "He who overcomes, I will grant to him to sit down with Me on My throne, as I also overcame and sat down with My Father on His throne" (Rev. 3:21 NASB).

"Everyone born of God overcomes the world. This is the victory that has overcome the world, even our faith" (1 John 5:4). *Overcome* is translated from a Greek word that depicts an athlete standing at the podium, receiving an award for victory. Get this: that Greek word translated "overcome" stems from the word *nike* and means "to carry off the victory."[2] For this reason, the largest athletic shoe manufacturer in the world used it as the name of its corporation.

Nike is more than a swoosh on a shoe: it implies a battle waged and won. As we've seen over the past few chapters, the Bible teaches Christians to recognize that the world is a battleground, not a playground. Jesus prepared us for a world filled with obstacles: spiritual warfare, temptation, persecution, and faith-testing seasons. But in the very same breath, He promised us we would "win life" if we stood firm in Him.

First of all, what are overcomers? Overcomers are followers of Christ who successfully resist the power and temptation of the world's system, their own flesh, and Satan's schemes. These are the Christ followers who choose to stand. Overcomers are not sinless but hold fast to faith in Christ until the end. They do not turn away when times get difficult or walk away when faith is tested.

One day at a ministry conference, the speaker held up an old black-and-white photo from his college days of five men, best friends, who had surrendered their lives to Jesus and to the ministry. The man holding the picture was around fifty years old at the time; three decades had passed since the photo was taken. He went into great detail to describe the passion each of his friends had for Christ and their earnest desire to leave a legacy for Him in their generation. Then he shocked his audience with these words: "Only two of the five still walk with Jesus today."

> Many will turn away from the faith and will betray and hate each other, and many false prophets will appear and deceive many people. Because of the increase of wickedness, the love of most will grow cold, but the one who stands firm to the end will be saved. (Matt. 24:10–13)

What happened to the three who fell away? How could it be that only two remained faithful? With pain in his voice, the speaker shared the story of seduction into sin that led one man down a road of destruction. Leaving his wife and his ministry, the man walked away from Christ to return to the darkness. The next man endured a faith-testing season that resulted in his forsaking his belief in God and turning to atheism. The last man—well, he became ensnared by the love of money, and his love for Jesus eventually grew cold.

Three men. Three struggles. Three who didn't stand.

Friends, the darkness, temptation, and persecution of the Enemy that we've looked at in this book have one purpose: to keep us from holding fast to Jesus. But the Bible says this: "Blessed is the one who perseveres under trial because, having stood the test, that person will receive the crown of life that the Lord has promised to those who love him" (James 1:12).

I write these words because I know the battle is real. In order for us to stand firm in this life, we must become men and women who fix our eyes on the heavenly goal. This world is temporary; eternity is forever. We must live for the day we will see Jesus face-to-face. When we maintain an eternal perspective, it shifts our gaze and keeps us running the race with perseverance.

I know from experience that falling away from the Lord is easy. I walked through a season of life that tested my faith severely. The sinister voice of the Enemy mocked my love for Jesus and tempted me to abandon my devotion. I'm forever grateful that the Lord opened my eyes in the midst of heartbreak to see Satan's agenda in my pain. What a blessing it is that the Word of God clearly conveys to us the Enemy's motive in tempting us to sin. Satan knows he can't change the status of our salvation as children of God, but he delights in thinking he can keep us from standing firm and receiving the rewards Jesus destined for us. Never forget, Satan is the one who came to "steal and kill and destroy" (John 10:10). He is the mastermind behind sin and suffering and seeks to use both to take away our eternal rewards.

My heart breaks over the stories I hear of ministry leaders falling or Christian families torn apart by sin. I know the Enemy revels in each of these falls, but the Lord has so much better for us. He has equipped us with everything we need to stand firm.

The Word of God is rich with promises to those who resist the pull of the Enemy and overcome. The apostle Paul wrote to the church in Corinth, "Stand firm. Let nothing move you. Always give yourselves fully to the work of the Lord, because you know that your labor in the Lord is not in vain" (1 Cor. 15:58). Friends, your perseverance in trials, your steadfastness in hope, and your resistance to temptation are not in vain. Jesus sees your faithfulness and will greatly reward you for standing firm!

LIVING FOR ETERNAL REWARDS

As a woman who spends much of her life on airplanes, I've noticed a pattern: the more I fly, the more rewards I receive. Airlines, credit card companies, and even Starbucks—they all know we are highly motivated by rewards. Therefore, they build elaborate systems to hook our loyalty.

Call me a sucker, but I'm living proof the system works.

For example, I work hard to maintain my status with a particular airline because I know that if I do so, I get perks. And by perks I mean sweet little extras that make the hassle of flying a little more comfortable. When you travel as much as I do, any little treat is a blessing. So when booking flights, I go out of my way to make sure to fly this particular airline so I can increase my miles. Why? Because I believe the promises made by the company: promises of better seats. Promises of free bag checking. Promises of better flight options. Oh yeah, and promises of better food. Can I get an amen?

Did you know Jesus made very similar promises? I guess you could say He established the very first incentive program. The theme of eternal rewards is repeated throughout the New Testament. Our motivation to stand firm today is because there are mind-blowing honors and blessings for the one who holds fast to Jesus.

It is written:

> "What no eye has seen,
>   what no ear has heard,
> and what no human mind has conceived"—
>   the things God has prepared for those
>   who love him. (1 Cor. 2:9)

Before we get into the nitty-gritty of the different rewards in heaven, let's clarify the big difference between judgment for sin and judgment for rewards. As Christ followers, the penalty for our sin was paid in full by Jesus on the cross. Because of His righteousness, we stand before God completely forgiven. Therefore, when we die, we will not stand before God to be judged for our sin. That judgment is reserved for nonbelievers and is called the great white throne judgment. The book of Revelation describes it in detail:

> I saw a great white throne and him who was seated on it. The earth and the heavens fled from his presence, and there was no place for them. And I saw the dead, great and small, standing before the throne, and books were opened. Another book was opened, which is the book of life. The dead were judged according to what they had done as recorded in the books. The sea gave up the dead that were in it, and death and Hades gave up the dead that were in them, and each person was judged according to what they had done. Then death and Hades were thrown into the lake of fire. The lake of fire is the second death. Anyone whose name was not found written in *the book of life* was thrown into the lake of fire. (20:11–15)

The key difference between the two judgments is whether one's name is found in the Book of Life. When we trust Jesus as Savior, our names are listed as evidence that we are children of God. Therefore, our judgment is different and is called the judgment seat of Christ: "We must all appear before *the judgment seat of Christ*, so that each of us may receive what is due us for the things done while in the body, whether good or bad" (2 Cor. 5:10).

The term *judgment seat* is translated from the Greek word *bema*, which, in its simplest definition, describes a place reached by steps, or a platform. In Greek culture, bema referred to the raised platform before which victorious athletes stood to receive their crowns. The Bible depicts a scene much like the one we witness at the Olympic Games. At the bema, children of God will take their places before Christ and there receive crowns and rewards based on their lives on earth.

Once again, this bears repeating: this judgment does not determine salvation; rather, it is when believers will give accounts of their lives to Christ. At the bema, Christ will bring to light every deed—good or bad—that believers have done on earth since they became Christians. Every Christian will be rewarded based on words, deeds, and faithfulness. Theologian Donald Grey Barnhouse wrote,

> Let us live, then, in the light of eternity. If we do not, we are weighting the scales against our eternal welfare…. Every thought and intent of the heart will come under the scrutiny of the Lord and His coming. We can be sure that at the Judgment Seat of Christ there will be a marked difference between the Christian who has lived his life before the Lord, clearly discerning what was for the glory of God, and another Christian who was saved in a rescue mission at the tag end of a depraved and vicious life, or a nominal Christian saved on his deathbed after a life of self-pride, self-righteousness, self-love, and self-sufficiency. All will be in heaven, but the differences will be eternal. We may be sure that the

consequences of our character will survive the grave and that we shall face those consequences at the Judgment Seat of Christ.[3]

HOW WE STAND DETERMINES ETERNAL REWARDS

Why is it so easy for us to comprehend rewards when it comes to earthly things like airline miles and free coffee but so easy for us to forget when it comes to our eternal destiny? Our time on earth is a mere vapor in comparison to our heavenly home. I think it is high time we took seriously the words of Scripture:

> Do not store up for yourselves treasures on earth, where moths and vermin destroy, and where thieves break in and steal. But *store up for yourselves treasures in heaven*, where moths and vermin do not destroy, and where thieves do not break in and steal. For where your treasure is, there your heart will be also. (Matt. 6:19–21)

> Do you not know that in a race all the runners run, but only one gets the prize? *Run in such a way as to get the prize.* Everyone who competes in the games goes into strict training. They do it to get a crown that will not last, but we do it to get a crown that will last forever. Therefore I do not run like someone running aimlessly; I do not fight like a boxer beating the air. No, I strike

a blow to my body and make it my slave so that
after I have preached to others, I myself will not
be disqualified for the prize. (1 Cor. 9:24–27)

I have a precious friend and mentor named Dr. Jim DeLoach. He is ninety-three years young today. Brother Jim, as many call him, is my spiritual grandfather and one of the greatest influences on my life. We taught Bible study together for years, and I've stood in awe as he's served the Lord through illnesses, heartbreak, and myriads of life changes. His faithfulness has modeled for me what it means to stand firm till the end.

Dr. DeLoach trusted Jesus as Savior while he was a soldier serving in World War II. As a teenager, he committed his life to Christ, and more than seven decades later, this man of God still loves and serves Jesus like no one else I know. Without a shadow of a doubt, he will stand before the throne of God one day and hear Him say, "Well done, good and faithful servant!" (Matt. 25:21).

Now that we live in different cities, I only get to talk to my friend about once a month. But when I do get to spend some time with him, he passes on pearls of wisdom. I asked him one day what the secret is to standing firm for a lifetime. He smiled and with his deep southern drawl simply said, "Marian, don't ever take your eyes off Jesus."

As I chewed on his wise words, I thought back to Moses and the others we've studied in this book. The one thing that kept those heroes of the faith standing firm in the midst of darkness, temptation, and persecution was where they had fixed their eyes. Just as an Olympic athlete trains and perseveres through challenges, with eyes fixed on the prize, so do we! Moses was able to stand firm at the Red Sea only because his gaze was firmly fixed on God's glorious presence instead of his circumstances. Paul taught us to stand firm against the forces of darkness by focusing on Jesus's triumphant victory over Satan. And we can't forget the words of John that tell us we can stand in the face of persecution only by abiding in Christ and remaining steadfast in His presence. We stand against every storm by planting our feet on Jesus, the Solid Rock.

> Since we are surrounded by such a great cloud of witnesses, let us throw off everything that hinders and the sin that so easily entangles. And let us run with perseverance the race marked out for us, *fixing our eyes on Jesus,* the pioneer and perfecter of faith. For the joy set before him he endured the cross, scorning its shame, and sat down at the right hand of the throne of God. (Heb. 12:1–2)

When Jesus gathered His disciples together and prepared them for the difficult times to come, He gave this magnificent promise: "Stand firm, and you will win life" (Luke 21:19). Scripture tells us to expect dark days, seasons of testing, persecution, and doubt in which our faith is put through the fire. Over the course of this book, we've studied what it means for us to stand firm.

The call to stand firm is synonymous in Scripture with our spiritual maturity and the fortitude of faith that resists temptation, perseveres through trials, and remains faithful when persecuted. As believers, we learn to stand by having to stand. Only when the waves of doubt, fear, temptation, and accusation assail us do we exercise our spiritual muscles and hold our ground.

The Bible is clear on this fact: our Enemy is defeated. When we stand firm, we proclaim by our faith-filled posture that we know Jesus is victorious. Unmoved, unshaken, and unstoppable are the people of God who truly believe. The kingdom of God advances mightily with bold warriors who walk by faith and hold their ground of victory. Likewise, the kingdom of darkness quakes in fear that the church would actually rise up and take a victorious position in Christ.

Therefore, let us rise up and take our stand.

- We are not victims.
- We are not defeated.
- We are not overwhelmed.
- We are more than conquerors.

In whatever tests, trials, and temptations we face, our God will triumph. We can stand firm, knowing the scoreboard doesn't define our destinies. Although the darkness may at times appear to be winning, we know the truth. It is my earnest prayer that when you face the fiercest attacks of darkness, one all-surpassing truth will ring in your heart: "He's got this!"

Friends, we stand firm because Jesus wins!

> Till He returns or calls me home—
> Here in the pow'r of Christ I'll stand.[4]

QUESTIONS FOR REFLECTION

INTRODUCTION: JESUS WINS

1. *Stand* opens with Jesus's clear promise of victory in the midst of darkness: "Stand firm, and you will win life" (Luke 21:19). Begin your time of reflection by reading Matthew 24:3–13 and Luke 21:8–19. How would you have felt as one of Jesus's disciples hearing about the difficult times to come? How does the clear promise of victory encourage your heart?

2. In what ways do you see similarities between the world Jesus described and our own?

3. What are some ways that you, as a Christ follower, feel pressure, temptation, fear, or persecution in today's culture?

4. In this section, we examined the story of Shadrach, Meshach, and Abednego, who were pressured to bow to a golden idol or face a fiery furnace. How can you relate to the temptation to conform to

culture? What is something you feel pressured to "bow down" to in this world rather than stand in allegiance to your faith?

5. This section closes with the story of Olympic gymnast Kerri Strug. Although she was down on the mat, she made the choice to rise up and stand. In what area of life do you most need to rise up and stand?

CHAPTER 1: STAND AND SEE

1. This chapter addresses the old cliché, "God will never give you more than you can handle." When has someone expressed this notion to you, or when have you believed it?

2. What characterizes a Red Sea moment?

3. We're hardwired for one of two things: fight or flight. Which are you more likely to do when faced with trials or challenges? How is the call to stand and see different?

4. Often we hear the word *stand* and think of our posture or position. But standing is a decision of the will more than just an external physical behavior. In what situation have you been called to stand?

5. In this chapter, we discovered that faith comes before sight. How does faith contradict emotions or reason?

CHAPTER 2: STAND IN AWE

1. This chapter examines our core beliefs about God's character. How do Red Sea moments expose what we truly believe about God's goodness, power, ability, and faithfulness?

2. In the journey of faith, one season prepares us to stand firm in the next. How did Moses's encounter with the Lord at the burning bush prepare him to stand firm at the Red Sea?

3. At the burning bush, the Lord revealed His holy name, I AM. How does this name of God speak to our fears and doubts?

4. I shared how my "faith muscles" grew as I faced different scenarios in which I was forced to believe God. How have your faith muscles grown stronger or weaker over time?

5. When we stand in awe of the Lord, we are prepared to face life's greatest challenges. How do authentic worship and a growing relationship with God fuel faith that withstands life's storms?

CHAPTER 3: HE'S GOT THIS

1. This chapter teaches that faith is choosing to believe "He's got this." How does believing this truth affect your mind, will, and emotions in a crisis or challenging circumstance?

2. Take a few minutes to read the dramatic story of God's deliverance of His people in Exodus 14:19–31. What is the most meaningful part of the story to you? Why?

3. What role did God's presence (the cloud by day and fire by night) play in the deliverance of His people?

4. Jesus's name is *Emmanuel* ("God with us"). How does knowing that God's presence is always with you enable you to stand?

5. When have you sensed God's empowering presence when you were too weak to stand on your own? How did that experience change you?

6. This chapter examines how the Lord fights for His people so He alone can be glorified. What are some ways we can interfere with His work? How is the Lord asking you to stand and see Him accomplish His will in your life?

CHAPTER 4: ON CHRIST THE SOLID ROCK I STAND

1. This chapter turns our attention to where our feet are planted. Take a few minutes to read Matthew 7:24–27. Where are we supposed to stand?

2. What is the difference between the wise and the foolish builders in the passage? What do both have in common?

3. This chapter examines the "sinking sand" we are tempted to build our lives upon instead of building upon Christ, the Solid Rock. Examples of sinking sand include relationships, money, success, power, perfection, and religion. What pitfalls await those who choose to build upon these flimsy foundations?

4. What does it mean to be dressed in Jesus's righteousness and to be found "faultless to stand before the throne"? What images come to mind? How does the story of the prodigal son illustrate this truth?

5. Why is it imperative that we plant our feet firmly on Jesus and His righteousness if we are going to stand firm in this world?

CHAPTER 5: ALL OTHER GROUND IS SINKING SAND

1. Read the dramatic account of Peter's encounter with Jesus in Luke 5:1–11. What was Peter's response to Jesus's words? How did this response change his life?

2. According to the teaching in this chapter, what is a disciple? When did you first commit your life to follow Jesus and obey His teachings?

3. In this chapter, we discovered that standing firm requires not only intellectual belief in Christ but also commitment to living out His teachings. How does your obedience testify to your faith?

4. Why can't we separate faith from obedience to God's Word?

5. Take a minute to read 2 Timothy 4:3–4. How do these verses describe the world in which we live today? How are you called to stand in this culture as a Christ follower?

6. In this chapter, we saw that God is good and that obeying His commandments brings blessing. How does believing God is good prove essential to a life of obedience?

CHAPTER 6: STAND FIRM AGAINST THE WAVES

1. Our lives as Christ followers can feel much like standing against crashing waves. How can you relate to this analogy? What types of waves typically knock you down?

2. Take a few minutes to read and reflect on 1 Peter 5:8. Would you say you are aware or unaware of spiritual warfare? Explain.

3. Read John 8:44. Who did Jesus call our Enemy? What specific lies or deceptions have you believed about yourself, God, or life in general? What is Satan's agenda in speaking these lies?

4. Page 129 lists the various types of waves or mental assaults the Enemy employs against us. Take a few minutes to read this list. Which of the "waves" have you experienced?

5. In this chapter, I shared a very personal story of a spiritual attack on my mind. Flooded by thoughts of rejection, my emotions spiraled. How can you relate to this story?

6. Worship proved the key to victory over the darkness. What worship song or hymn helps you stand firm when the lies descend? Which specific lines speak to you?

CHAPTER 7: EQUIPPED FOR VICTORY

1. This chapter opens with a summary of the life of the apostle Paul. Why is he a good person to teach us how to stand? Who in your life has taught you about standing firm in the face of darkness, temptation, or persecution? How?

2. Take a few minutes to read Ephesians 6:10–17. Why does this passage call us to stand, and what is the result of our obedience?

3. The first piece of armor examined in this chapter is the belt of truth. Why is this piece essential? How does it enable us to stand firm?

4. Next we examined the breastplate of righteousness. Explain the difference between imputed and practiced righteousness. Why are both essential to victory?

5. Take a few minutes to read Ephesians 4:22–27. How does sin or rebellion give the Devil opportunity to torment or harass us?

6. One of Satan's chief strategies against Christ followers is to rob us of peace. How does experiencing the love of God enable us to stand firm against spiritual warfare?

CHAPTER 8: RESIST HIM!

1. What is the difference between a passive and an active faith? How can you engage with truth rather than just know truth?

2. The shield of faith is given to us to protect us from the fiery darts of the Evil One. We saw several examples of this type of warfare on pages 162–63. How have you experienced this type of attack?

3. According to the teaching in this chapter, how does the shield of faith extinguish Satan's fiery darts?

4. Nothing proves more vital to our ability to stand firm than knowing our identity as children of God. Take a few minutes to read the chart on page 169 that describes the difference between a "slave to sin" mind-set and a "child of God" mind-set. Which of the two mind-sets do you most often have about yourself? Why?

5. We are most vulnerable to the Enemy's attacks through our broken places. I shared my personal story of abuse and how it wreaked havoc on my identity. Is there any place of wounding or pain from your past that the Enemy still uses to access your life today? What is it?

6. What is the sword of the Spirit, and how does it give us victory over the Enemy? How did Jesus demonstrate this offensive weapon for us?

7. Read 1 John 4:4. How does this truth encourage your heart?

CHAPTER 9: STAND WHEN THE WORLD HATES YOU

1. Persecution is a reality for Christians across the globe. Take a few minutes to pray for our brothers and sisters in Christ who are enduring much hostility from the Evil One. (For tips on how to pray, visit www.persecution.com.)

2. Read John 15:18–21 and 16:1–4. Jesus warned us that we will be persecuted for our faith. Why is this warning a good thing? When have you felt like an outsider because of your faith in Christ? How does this warning keep believers from falling away?

3. To stand firm in the face of persecution, Jesus said we must abide in Him. How does a personal and close relationship with Christ enable us to withstand the anger, insults, harassment, or harm that will come our way because of our faith?

4. Romans 12:14 instructs us to bless those who persecute us. What is the purpose of blessing them? Read Proverbs 25:21. In what tangible ways are we called to respond when persecuted?

5. How does the call to rejoice when persecuted seem illogical? What is the real reason we rejoice?

6. Spend some time praying for strength to stand strong in the face of ridicule, anger, or persecution.

CHAPTER 10: WIN LIFE!

1. This chapter opens with the story of Olympian Wilma Rudolf. What are some words you would use to describe someone who overcomes?

2. Jesus prepared us for a world filled with obstacles: spiritual warfare, temptation, persecution, and faith-testing seasons. But in the very same breath, He promised we would "win life" if we stand firm in Him. Read James 1:12. How does this promise to overcomers convict, challenge, or encourage you?

3. What are some reasons people fall away from Christ and don't stand firm?

4. This chapter discusses how eternal rewards motivate us to hold fast to Jesus. What are some other ways "rewards" motivate you (e.g., airlines, Starbucks)? Why does it prove easier to believe in earthly rewards than heavenly ones?

5. Read Matthew 6:19–21. How can you better believe and apply this command today?

6. Think back through the heroes of faith we studied in this book. What do they all hold in common? How does their faith inspire your own?

7. Conclude your time of reflection by praying for increased faith in God, devotion to His Word, and resolve to stand in your generation.

ACKNOWLEDGMENTS

I owe a huge debt of gratitude to the following people for their love, support, wisdom, and prayers in the writing of *Stand*.

To the amazing team at the Fedd Agency: Thank you for championing this message! Esther, your leadership is unparalleled.

To Rebecca and Emily: Thank you for serving alongside me at Redeemed Girl and for your constant encouragement along the way. There have been some crazy days in this process, and I'm so grateful for how you've persevered and kept all the plates spinning.

To the RGM board of directors: I am forever grateful for your covering, leadership, and vision as we seek to see a generation redeemed for His glory.

To Tonya, John, and Megan: Thank you for reading the manuscript. Your feedback throughout this process was a game changer! I'm so blessed by your friendship and how you live out this message so beautifully.

To all the incredible folks at David C Cook: I'm so blessed to work with a team who believes that God's Word transforms lives. Tim Peterson, you are the best editor! I am thankful for your honest feedback and genuine heart for Christ.

To the Jordan and Ellis families: I've watched you stand and believe God in the face of many trials and storms. Thank you for modeling faith that stands firm! Ralph and Patty, you've held your ground against cancer, and your journey of faith inspires many. Mom, thank you for constantly studying God's Word and supplying me with fresh insights into the word *stand*. Dad, thank you for believing God and not bowing down to the pharaohs of this world.

To Andrew and Brenden, my incredible bonus boys: Your faith in Jesus at such young ages leaves me speechless. I believe God is doing a beautiful thing in your generation, and I can't wait to see how He calls and equips you to stand for Him. Your prayers over this book have meant the world to me. I love you!

To Sydney: You've been my little cowriter throughout this process, especially from the womb. Thanks for awakening me in the middle of the night so I could crank out a few more pages. God works all things for His good and glory, and I believe the miracle of your life as I birthed this message was no accident. Knowing you would enter this world inspired me to see decades ahead and believe that "Jesus wins." As I hold you in my arms today, I pray your faith in God and devotion to Jesus keep you standing firm in Him.

To the love of my life and my ministry partner, Justin: We are better together. You've taught me to stand and see. I am still in awe of how God brought us together for the glory of His name. Thank you for living every word of this book with me. I love you.

Visit www.standbiblestudy.com for teaching
videos, small-group materials, and more!

NOTES

INTRODUCTION

1. Rick Weinberg, "Kerri Strug Fights Off Pain, Helps U.S. Win Gold," *ESPN*, July 19, 2004, www.espn.com/espn/espn25/story?page=moments/51.

2. Weinberg.

3. Weinberg.

CHAPTER 1: STAND AND SEE

1. Steven Furtick, "Your Faith. God's Faithfulness," ChurchLeaders.com, October 20, 2011, http://churchleaders.com/pastors/pastor-blogs/155702-steven_furtick_your _faith_gods_faithfulness.html.

CHAPTER 2: STAND IN AWE

1. Roy and Revel Hession, *We Would See Jesus* (Fort Washington, PA: Christian Literature Crusade, 1958), 25.

CHAPTER 3: HE'S GOT THIS

1. Hillsong United, "The Stand (Live)," *United We Stand (Live)* © 2010 Hillsong Church.

CHAPTER 4: ON CHRIST THE SOLID ROCK I STAND

1. Edward Mote, "My Hope Is Build on Nothing Less," *Trinity Hymnal*, rev. ed. (Suwanee, GA: Great Commission, 1998),521.

CHAPTER 5: ALL OTHER GROUND IS SINKING SAND

1. Keith Krell, "Storm Warning (Matthew 7:24–29)," Bible.org, March 23, 2010, https://bible.org/seriespage/12-storm-warning-matthew-724-29.

2. W. E. Vine, *Vine's Expository Dictionary of New Testament Words* (Zeeland, MI: Reformed Church, 2015), 2:170.

CHAPTER 6: STAND FIRM AGAINST THE WAVES

1. Chip Ingram, *The Invisible War: What Every Believer Needs to Know about Satan, Demons, and Spiritual Warfare* (Grand Rapids, MI: Baker Books, 2006), 44.

2. Steven J. Cole, "Lesson 55: Standing Strong, Standing Firm (Ephesians 6:10–11)," Bible.org, 2008, https://bible.org/book/export/html/22076.

3. Ingram, *Invisible War*, 28.

4. Tony Brown and Pat Barrett, "Good Good Father," *Housefires II* © 2014 Housefires.

CHAPTER 9: STAND WHEN THE WORLD HATES YOU

1. "Syria: I Am N," *The Voice of the Martyrs*, October 13, 2015, www.persecution.com /public/newsroom.aspx?story_ID==373837.

2. Morgan Lee, "Sorry, Tertullian: Recent Research Tests the Most Famous Adage about the Persecuted Church," *Christianity Today*, December 4, 2014, www.christianitytoday.com/ct/2014/december/sorry-tertullian.html.

CHAPTER 10: WIN LIFE!

1. "Wilma Rudolph Biography," *Encyclopedia of World Biography*, www.notablebiographies .com/RO-Sc/Rudolph-Wilma.html.

2. "Nikaó," Bible Hub, http://biblehub.com/greek/3528.htm.

3. Donald Grey Barnhouse, quoted in Randy Alcorn, *Money, Possessions, and Eternity* (Carol Stream, IL: Tyndale, 1989), 120–21.

4. Keith Getty and Stuart Townend, "In Christ Alone"(c) 2001 Kingsway Thankyou Music.

Visit **www.standbiblestudy.com** for teaching videos, small-group materials, and more!